FENG SHUI

Creating Abundance in Your Home With Feng Shui

(Feng Shui Guidelines for Keeping a Check on Your Greens Indoor)

Heather Davis

Published By **Heather Davis**

Heather Davis

All Rights Reserved

Feng Shui: Creating Abundance in Your Home With Feng Shui (Feng Shui Guidelines for Keeping a Check on Your Greens Indoor)

ISBN 978-1-77485-441-9

All rights reserved. No part of this guide may be reproduced in any form without permission in writing from the publisher except in the case of brief quotations embodied in critical articles or reviews.

Legal & Disclaimer

The information contained in this book is not designed to replace or take the place of any form of medicine or professional medical advice. The information in this book has been provided for educational and entertainment purposes only.

The information contained in this book has been compiled from sources deemed reliable, and it is accurate to the best of the Author's knowledge; however, the Author cannot guarantee its accuracy and validity and cannot be held liable for any errors or omissions. Changes are periodically made to this book. You must consult your doctor or get professional medical advice before using any of the suggested remedies, techniques, or information in this book.

Upon using the information contained in this book, you agree to hold harmless the Author from and against any damages, costs, and expenses, including any legal fees potentially resulting from the application of any of the information provided by this guide. This disclaimer applies to any damages or injury caused by the use and application, whether directly or indirectly, of any advice or information presented, whether for breach of contract, tort, negligence, personal injury, criminal intent, or under any other cause of action.

You agree to accept all risks of using the information presented inside this book. You need to consult a professional medical practitioner in order to ensure you are both able and healthy enough to participate in this program.

TABLE OF CONTENTS

INTRODUCTION 1

CHAPTER 1: WHAT ARE THE PRINCIPLES OF FENG SHUI 3

CHAPTER 2: MAPPING YOUR OFFICE USING BAGUA 7

CHAPTER 3: ARRANGE YOUR OFFICE 12

CHAPTER 4: FENG SHUI WORK HABITS 22

CHAPTER 5: FENG SHUI COLORS 29

CHAPTER 6: GENERAL FENG SHUI TIPS 33

CHAPTER 7: A QUICK HISTORY OF FENG SHUI.................. 37

CHAPTER 8: THE LIVING ROOM 46

CHAPTER 9: UNDERSTANDING FENG SHUI....................... 70

CHAPTER 10: GUIDE TO FENG SHUI LIVING ROOM DECOR 80

CHAPTER 11: PROPER FENG SHUI LIVING ROOM LAYOUT 83

CHAPTER 12: STEPS IN GOOD LIVING ROOM FENG SHUI . 91

CHAPTER 13: BEST FENG SHUI LIVING ROOM COLORS 97

CHAPTER 14: TIPS ON PROPER LIVING ROOM FENG SHUI 101

CHAPTER 15: TOP 28 WEALTH FENG SHUI TIPS FOR YOUR HOME! 109

CHAPTER 16: HOW TO MAKE YOUR OWN PROSPERITY JAR! ! 118

CHAPTER 17: VISION BOARD INSTRUCTIONS FOR THE VISION BOARD 120

CHAPTER 18: THE 1000 THANK-YOU CHALLENGE 123

CHAPTER 19: HERE ARE 35 STEPS TO REDUCE YOUR MONTHLY EXPENSES FROM TODAY! 124

CHAPTER 20: MIND SET AND THE LAW OF ATTRACTION! 136

CHAPTER 21: GOAL SETTING TIPS 145

CHAPTER 22: THE POWER OF CRYSTAL GEMSTONES 148

CHAPTER 23: CLEANING YOUR GEMSTONES 158

CHAPTER 24: REASONS WHY WE REQUIRE FENG SHUI .. 161

CHAPTER 25: USING FENG SHUI TO COMPLETELY ELIMINATE OBSTACLESIN YOUR LIFE 174

CONCLUSION 184

Introduction

This book outlines practical steps and strategies for how to achieve peace confidence, success, and peace by utilizing the old principles of Feng Shui!

In the following chapters, you'll be taught about the concept of feng shui what it is, how it works and how you can apply it to improve your working life. Do you realize that most prestigious businesses and corporations throughout China in addition to Japan employ feng-shui experts together with architects when they plan their international business centres? Are you aware that many of the top businesspeople worldwide adhere to the principles of feng Shui?

This book can help you understand why they were successful, and provides strategies that you can easily copy to accomplish similar. It doesn't matter if work in a cubicle , from your home, or run an individual business or a huge company.

The power of balancing feng the shui is universal and will be beneficial to you.

Thanks for downloading the book and I hope you'll thoroughly enjoy it!

Chapter 1: What Are The Principles Of Feng Shui

Feng Shui is an ancient Chinese philosophy which could possibly go to around four thousand B.C., given current evidence of prehistoric structures as well burial rituals. It describes the interactions between the person and their surroundings and energy flow, or energy or chi that runs through everything.

In essence Feng shui examines how certain patterns forms, colors, and even directions alter our behavior and think on a deeper instinctual level. It has identified certain philosophical concepts that people who are successful use to enhance their actions as well as their businesses.

If you adhere to these guidelines and practices, you'll be able help to facilitate to bring qi or energy, through your business and work life, and also eliminate energy blockages or issues prior to them affecting your business!

The Three Principles

Feng Shui is based on three fundamental principles. Whatever method or scheme you decide to use for your house, you should keep these fundamental principles in mind and consider how they affect the way you work and how you believe about work.

1. Every single thing in the universe is alive. Everything we see including the chair our bodies, as well as the outside world, are comprised of constant energetic, moving energy as quantum mechanics confirm. In addition, our thoughts and emotions are composed of energy. If we are either sad or happy in certain circumstances, then we typically be feeling the same way in similar situations.

2. All things in the universe are connected. On a fundamental level, this implies that energy flows across all objects and it's only at the'macro-level which we perceive them as separate objects. At a higher level, this also implies that everything you

do in your office is linked with you and your achievement as well as your self-worth and your personal life and even your emotions. Similar to this the holidays, your childhood as well as your future are connected to every other aspect that you live. Utilizing feng Shui and feng shui, you can leverage this connection to your advantage and let your good memories and natural strengths boost your growth in your business.

3. Everything changes. This is the essence of Feng Shui, and the concept of movement. There is no one fixed strategy to succeed however, we have to always changing, adapting and shifting energy around. If we're unhappy or feel frustrated or unable to move forward the reason is usually because we need to learn to be flexible and adaptable!

It is the art and science to bring these 3 concepts to a state of equilibrium. You may be wondering what this is to do with your professional life, but take a look at the way your life's emotional state is linked to your work surroundings:

* What are your feelings about your office?

What is your first reaction when you know you're required to go to work every morning?

Are there areas of the workplace that you love or do you dislike others?

* What is the predominant feeling you get when working the office?

You'll soon realize that your mood and Qi or energy actually have a significant impact on your work life andperhaps even affecting the success or failure of your business!

Chapter 2: Mapping Your Office Using Bagua

As feng shui experts are employed to examine the entire structure, you need to be able to map the office area you have.

The Bagua Directions

The bagua directions are also known as They are built on the principles of the ancient manual for divination called The I Ching and correspond to the areas of your life. When you map out your "life at work and home, you can help connect your work and family life, creating an environment that is peaceful, balanced. Keep in mind that the aim of Feng Shui is to live an uncluttered, peaceful, and harmonious lifewhere each part of you is supportive and helping the others!

Draw a simple rectangle or square that represents the office space. Even if your office isn't square, these spaces will indicate which'section of your space you are in control of and can be changed.

Divide into 9 equal boxes. Three across the top, and three down the sides. Then, number each box 1-9 as the way.

1, 2, 3

4, 5, 6

7, 8, 9

* Underneath the row at the bottom (7 8, 9) Write the word "Entrance. The door to your office is located it will be aligned in this manner. The goal is to attract the right energy to your office through that entry point to the appropriate zones. By moving your desk or other furniture for your office You will notice that you can improve the flow of energy around your office.

* Record the significance of each space below and then use some of the suggestions to anchor positive energy to the rooms:

1. Prosperity and wealth

Purple is a color that represents extravagant objects, and the richness.

Items that relate to your wealth, such as bank files or a secure. Green, healthy round-leafed plants.

2. Fame and repute

Art, sayings and quotations about achievement. Show any certificates, awards or awards here. Utilize the color red for things that are related to the fire, sun, or passion.

3. Marriage, love and relationships

A set of connected items like vases or decorations. Things that promote communication like phones or fax machines.

4. Friends, family and health

Family items like photographs, artwork or even flowers.

5. Grounding and centering

Make use of the space to make it more open or items that are of a yellow or earth tone color, solid, or rectangular.

6. Creativity and children

Items that are playful and whimsical with white or pastel. It could be a token toys or an image that appears exuberant and fun.

7. Self-cultivation and knowledge

Plants that are healthy and robust in bookshelves that are adorned with vibrant shades like greens and blues (not yellows or reds). Columns, stripes and straight items that go up and down.

8. Career

Crystal or glass objects reflecting your work as well as what you do, as reflections of art or water. reflections of water.

9. Travel and friendly people

Images of your team members as well as your clients and inspiring mentors. Maybe filing cabinets that include your client list , or even contacts in the business.

The Work Desk and Directions for Bagua

If your office space is only your desk at work, then you could apply the same guidelines there too. For instance, you may prefer to put the computer's monitor in your wealth zone (the rear left) or place your notebook and laptop on the right side of your professional space. The plaque with your name or award in the center (fame) as well as photos of your partner in the love space (back left).

Chapter 3: Arrange Your Office

Entrance

The first step you should follow after planning your workplace is to look at the entrance. Are you able to see your professional life, helpful individuals or areas of expertise? Ideally, it should open directly into your area of expertise, right the front the desk. However, based on the nature of your business, you might prefer to open it to the area of helpful employees (if you have lots of customers) or know-how (if your business is dependent on the gathering and consolidation of information).

Make sure the opening is as large and accessible as you can, so that you don't block the flow of energy that is needed to move between the office and outside. Be sure to keep clutter in your office!

Desk Placement

The desk at your office is the centerpiece of your office. It is the place you would like the most effective energy to flow to and be anchored to. There are a lot of vital fengshui strategies to make use of when arranging your office.

In the opposite direction to the entrance

This allows you to take a position of control over the room (it is also helpful because it's located in the bagua of fame and wealth).

Removing from the Back Wall

There must be plenty of room for movement and space in between your and the wall behind If not, you'll become a bit trapped and your business may cease to appreciate new opportunities.

Do not turn your back to the door

This can result in you losing your focus frequently and become awestruck by the new opportunities or arrivals. If you can't keep your back from the door, be sure to look out over your front door, such as by using a mirror or an image frame that is reflective. A mirror that allows the user with a clear view of what's going on behind you could be helpful!

You should have the Big Enough Desk

Use a wider desk if you can. This will provide you with the room and the space you need to be creative and free. Maintain it clean throughout the day and carry along medals, awards, trophies or other symbols of your accomplishments.

Your Chair

Check that your seat or the "throne" that you have in your space is comfortable and ergonomic. This piece of furniture serves as the primary support you need and, in turn, your business. It should be secure and comfortable every time you place your feet on it.

Balancing Office Furniture

It is essential to maintain the overall style of your office space by choosing the proper dimensions of furniture and making sure they complement one another. This will allow your energy flow easily and promote a calm environment, not unsettling pieces of furniture that attract attention or distract it.

* If you're in an office that is small and you are not able to use large furniture. Make sure you use a discrete tall filing cabinet and then reduce them!

* If you have a large office make sure you use a desk that is small since this could devalue the person working behind it.

When you've got windows in your workplace, do not block it with a wall or hide it behind furniture. Remember that you're looking for the energy of the new sunlight shining through and lighting your hard work!

Room Form

A very prevalent Feng Shui problems that affect peace of mind in the office is the formal office shape that is not situated in square, oval or rectangle. If the shape of the room isn't ideal (and the majority of offices are in this day and age of office spaces that are squeezed) This can affect how energy circulates through the space and ultimately the way you work.

If your office is a bit oddly shaped (liken it is situated in the middle of the heating or plumbing pipes, or have strange spaces and nooks everywhere) Expect problems and delays to your work routinely.

* Make use of mirrors, draperies and tapestries to conceal the imperfections and to reflect or highlight the areas you would like to draw attention to.

Unwanted Posts, Columns, and Projected Corners

If your workplace has these types of items that disrupt an otherwise smooth flow in your plan for bagua take the opportunity to ward off the energy loss by purchasing the largest healthy plant and placing it over or on top of the object that has caused the problem.

Sharp Angles

Edges and sharp angles of cabinets, desks, or any other furniture can cause tension and confusion creating a fracture and cutting your energy flow when it attempts to move from one part of the room to the next.

Make sure to purchase furniture with corners that are rounded.

Cover sharp corners with or hangings, plants or attractive shades.

Glass Walls

Although plastic or glass screens are commonplace in modern offices however, they are negative for fengshui since they promote the illusion of space and movement even though you're actually in a tight space. Many people feel trapped when they are confined in this manner.

Blinds or drapes to draw attention to the glass surfaces to give you the feeling of belonging to your own space and also strengthening the boundaries.

Lighting

As with most office workers, you'll discover that florescent lighting is not the most productive working environment. The most effective light source is sunlight that is infused with the natural energy of qi which is the energy we were born to be able to absorb.

Always make sure to install full-spectrum bulbs or daylight bulbs whenever it is possible. They are at a minimum, they provide the closest thing to natural lighting that can be found inside the office.

Make use of additional lighting, like lamps, a small bars or reading lamps on your desk. Also, make sure to use only daylight bulbs or full-spectrum bulbs.

Cubicle Living

Applying the principles of feng Shui for a cubicle is much more challenging than applying them for an office, however with these current times of economic recession and mass unemployment, often we're stuck with our working schedules. But, you'll be relieved to be aware that there are options to consider.

The simple cubicle is a poor design for an individual worker and makes them feel vulnerable and cut away from allies. The space surrounding them is not theirs it is not designed to the needs of their employees but is open for anyone to access.

The first step is to introduce living energy to your cubicle. This can be done through using healthy green-leafed, healthy plants (not Cactuses). It is crucial to use an odd, not an even number since odd numbers provide greater amount of energy and are more active than those 'stable' numbers.

Include a picture of water flowing (the bigger the more impressive) close to the door to your room as is possible. Since most cubicles don't have facilities for installing water fountains Instead, a photo (one that you took yourself) will help diffuse negative energy and help to encourage positive ones.

Plants and Aquariums

Aquariums and plants are essential elements to any office or, if you have a room or cubicle. They naturally contain well-maintained, clean living energy and bring a positive and healthy look to your space:

Fish tanks and aquariums are symbols of water, water moving and the cleansing power it exerts on Qi. Water is the most natural luck factor in feng shui , and cleansing.

* You can make use of plants or fish tanks as well as aquariums to disguise other less attractive features or to secure good energy in certain areas in the room. You could conceal an odd-shaped shape on your wealth map using plants, for instance or add luck to the location by adding an aquarium!

9. The plant of 9 and the 9 fish cure. This is among the most distinctive cures for Feng Shui and is a way to bring huge amounts of luck to your office. The day of the cure,

buy 9 healthy, new plants (and this cure works in similar to nine healthy fish) and place them the plants in your office in one go.

Chapter 4: Feng Shui Work Habits

Similar to how we've discussed before how important layout is for attract the right kind of energy to your workplace Next step is to review your working routines and routines. Remember the principle that everything is interconnected? It's truer than in a busy workplace, in which someone else's poor day could affect you and your productivity!

Boundaries

It is crucial to establish distinct physical and personal boundaries when working in a area. This lets you separate and shield your energy, qi and energy from disruptive or costly circumstances, which can impact the rest of your working day, or permanently impacting your happiness and your success at your work.

The workplace is an environment where you need to feel safe and secure, secure and secure in every aspect. This security foundation is what gives you confidence, and will allow you to take action and prudently. That is, you can make the right choices for your business! It can be difficult to make this happen if you feel you're in the hands of others.

Be sure that your room is separated. If you own your own space that's great - you can begin applying customized fengshui concepts immediately.

If you are in the same space, try to locate a method to clearly delineate your boundaries from the other's. You can use dividers however, you shouldn't intend to separate yourself from the rest of the world, only to increase the effect on your own energy. Utilize attractive or colorful plants to add a sense of beauty to your surroundings and also to protect yourself from other people. You'll soon realize that, when you do this, you'll prefer your workplace to your colleagues in the area, and you will begin to feel more relaxed.

- Personalize your space. Include family photos holiday, celebrations, or a memorable occasions.

* Add a healthy, green plant in your home to bring positivity and positive energy.

* Where possible, use color.

Organization

Decluttering is an important Feng Shui practice and your daily work practices have a significant impact on your performance and bringing peace to your workplace. Keep in mind the 3rd principle in feng-shui declares that everything is dynamic and evolving. If your living space is starting to fill up with static paper that has been untouched and won't move, it is likely that you're beginning becoming lost trapped in your home!

* Energy must allow to move through the office and circulate. It isn't able to do that in the event that you already have piles of unpaid bills or reports to read and unfinished work to finish!

A well-organized approach to your office involves regular cleaning, clear organizing guidelines, and being active in your surroundings. If you are engaged in your workplace, you're actively working on it, taking just only a few minutes each day clearing out the clutter, engaging, and allowing enthusiasm to run.

• Use a basic sorting system, regardless of whether it's an in or out tray or the filing cabinet. Make sure that everything is simple and a one task at a time. Don't let your bill pile to be your mail pile, your current reading pile, or even your door to shut!

* Try to arrange your office in accordance with bagua's guidelines. Documents should be kept strictly related to financial matters and also keep any new ideas blue-sky thinking, blue-sky ideas, and questions in your creative area.

* Take a chunk or time during the beginning of each day and then at the end of the day organizing. This will help open

the office to let in fresh enthusiasm, and also closing it down at the close of the day.

Make sure your desk is cleared whenever you can. If you have a tidy and well-lit space you're inviting energy to flow through.

Find the Right Time to Align Your Day

Make use of the rhythmic pattern of the day to ensure that you are following the fundamentals of feng Shui. The timings of the day's events have a major influence on the type of energy flows into your workplace and which tasks are most suitable for.

Morning

New ventures, imaginative tasks and brain mapping

Midday

Long-term customers, the mainstay of your company, is what your company excels at and gets the majority of its strength and support from

Afternoon

Long-haul work, breaking into the details of massive projects. Reports, bookkeeping and financials

Late Afternoon/End Of Day

Assessments or creativity, your workplace and colleagues

The Inner Work and Affirmations

It is also beneficial to employ feng shui along with affirmations as well as your own professional development activities to get the most of your workplace. Feng Shui should not only be restricted to not just your office space, but also your life. Think about these issues:

* Do you think you are successful?

Do you think you are to be content with your job?

* What goals for work have you set yourself in recent times?

Sample Feng Shui Affirmations

When you begin your working day begin by taking an instant to take a breath the first time you walk into your workspace for the day . You can think about or repeat in a calm manner any of these. Repeat the phrases three times:

I am at the center of my life. I am the creator of my own future.

I carry with me endless energy along with intelligence, skill, and determination.

If you feel scared or worried, or your emotional health has been damaged and you are unable to let that affect your Qi and disrupt your work tranquility, you can take a few moments to gaze out the window , and gently repeat to yourself one among the following

I am the outcome of a lifetime of beautiful, wild, and dramatic changes.

Although chaos could be all around me, I am in the peace of my center.

Chapter 5: Feng Shui Colors

Along with arranging your space and changing your habits of work and habits, you can boost the flow of positive energy throughout your workplace and promote peace while you achieve this by using positive colours. It's been long known by psychologists and counselors to have colors that hold a profound connection with the human mind. If this weren't an issue, film makers wouldn't earn as much income as they do today!

Colors can be associated with profound emotional states and associations in the mind. They are utilized to motivate or discourage certain mental states, feelings and habits of work.

Feng Shui Colors

If you are using colors with feng shui, then you may want to color directly areas of your office furniture or to include additional objects of the same color in a particular section on your map of bagua.

It is crucial that you match the correct colors to the correct regions of your map as well as your professional life. For instance, things in purple naturally correspond with fame and wealth areas.

Purple is the most ominous color in Feng Shui, it represents the wealth, opulence and respect. The color is thought to be an imperial or noble shade.

Red is a very fortunate, auspicious color that symbolizes joy, warm, and strength.

Green represents peace and health. It also represents hope, hope, and health. It is the representation of the earth and wood elements as well as all things that grow. The element can be used almost everywhere where there is a positive element.

Blue is a symbol of cleanliness, freshness and optimism.

The color black is a pity, as the color black symbolizes depression, negativity, and lack of positive energy. It shouldn't be utilized in Feng shui and should be avoided.

Gray is the colour of choice for the majority of offices is gray. It symbolizes discontent and is not a good choice for office spaces. It is vital to grade the color into more light, optimistic colors , or at the very least separated by the addition of green.

Brown is closely associated with earth respect, roots, and respect. It is a symbol of age and respect in an environment, and gives an impression of being solid and well-rooted.

Yellow/tan The color yellow symbolizes one of the Chinese symbol of hope and success and is typically seen close to the entrance or in an area where a brand new initiative is set to take off.

Orange is a symbol of power of happiness, joy, and prosperity, due to its similarity to the colour of the sun and to gold. It is a great way to bring success and positivity to the areas of Your bagua's map.

Notes on Office Colors

* When it comes to choosing colors for your office, a suitable overall color would be green because it symbolizes new growth and good fortune.

Try to align your office's colors with the company's, so your team's dynamic PR could contain an abundance of green, orange and red to symbolize the power of communication, health and enthusiasm.

Chapter 6: General Feng Shui Tips

Here is an overview of general Feng Shui techniques that you can apply today, now to improve your luck and bring peace into your workplace. They are organized in 'dos' and 'don'ts', so that you are able to clearly identify the steps to take.

Don'ts

Keep your body straight to the door, since it could cause you to be into the path of the incoming chaotic energy. Move slightly towards one side, and away from your position in the room.

* Turn your face towards to the right of doorway if working at home or in an office with a small staff. This is a symbol of attracting new energy and business to this location.

Do not look out of your workspace, so that you are looking straight into storage spaces, closets, or toilets because this only serves to focus your attention on difficult and ineffective spaces.

Dos

Place your computer in the north or west part of your office, to increase your creative abilities. Set your computer or laptop in the opposite direction to boost your earnings.

Keep your back to the wall to provide assistance (but keep in mind that you should have enough space for movement around you too).

If you are able, put your desk placed in the corner that is farthest from the entryway so you can take advantage of the command position.

Secure any safes to one of the two directions, either westward or northwest, as the element metal can be beneficial to financial security and wealth.

Make sure you have a balance of colors and yin Yang. If the color or object you are using is too strong, you can balance it out with a lighter, more delicate one, and the cycle continues. Finding the right pitch for harmony can help balance out the imbalances of energy.

• Keep the power cords on every piece of office equipment hidden out of view. This eliminates obstructions and allows the qi of the room to flow easily.

Be sure to treat your papers as well as files in the manner they merit. Maintain them in order and neat throughout the day, as they are a representation of your business and the clients it serves in the both present and future the past.

EMF (Electromagnetic Frequency) Radiation

You might want to look into EMF radiation as well as the radiation pulses that are released by all electronic devices (more than in older devices). In the modern workplace which is run largely through digital technology, this can be difficult to control in an office that is feng shui-friendly it might be beneficial to add additional plants (natural air purifiers) and salted-rock lighting (as they help to oxygenate your air). It is worth considering what you'll need in your office, and whether you'll need them all to be switched on during the day.

Feng Shui Home Life

We all know of, there are times when where and how we're working is a bit out of control and we must make the most possible use of the situation in a restricted way. It is important to remember that there is always a way to improve your natural chi in the most challenging circumstances. Think about the clothes you wear as well as the affirmations you use as well as your workplace space.

The lessons you've learned from this article can apply to personal or bedroom, so that you could use your space to recharge and unwind when your work life is stressful.

Chapter 7: A Quick History Of Feng Shui

Feng Shui has its roots in a variety of ancient philosophies, including Taoism, Confucianism, Buddhism, Shinto and Vashtu Shastri. The roots in Feng Shui can be traced back over 3,000 years to the rural areas of China. It is believed that it been developed by peasants in the early days when they were debating which place to build their houses, cultivate food crops and possibly most important, dig burial grounds. Each of these tasks was believed to require certain signs of the gods to determine the proper location.

When deciding on an area to build an apartment, they'd look for a river that is nearby and build the dwelling facing north. This means that they could enjoy warm sunshine in winter, and cool breezes during summer. In addition, when choosing the best location for a grave they would choose one that faces east to west and then place their bodies in a grave that was facing towards the west. Based on theories like the Yin and Yang theory east is a symbol of yang energy, and new life, while the west is a symbol of Yang energy and the older part of life. The concept that is now called Feng shui eventually emerged from these processes.

In the late nineteenth century, a man with the name Yang Yun-sung who is generally regarded as the Great Master of Feng Shui began teaching the significance of what he termed dragons energy, also known as dragon breath. This required careful analysis of the form of the landscape (mountains and hills, rivers and mountains) to identify areas that symbolized animals that were believed to be auspicious (dragons and tigers for instance). He taught that in these areas, there were huge levels of positive energy often referred to as Qi that were beneficial to human beings. The term was coined"form school" Feng shui (also often referred to as"the Landscape School).

About a century later, another school for feng-shui referred to in the Compass school was established under the direction of a man named Wang Chih. The compass school aimed to implement the principles of feng-shui across a range of flat landscapes. The name of the school suggests that this kind of feng shui utilizes a compass, as well as an instrument known as pakua or bagua. Baguas are essentially an feng shui-related map of your living space. The bagua is comprised of eight sections related to the different cardinal points (north south, east and northwest, west, northeast, northwest, southeast, and southwest). When used in conjunction, the bagua and compass enable users to increase the Qi within their surroundings.

The practice of feng Shui has been slowly and steadily developed through every generations of Chinese society. At one point , the number of people who practiced the art of feng shui was so large that whole cities could be planned and built based on its principles. However, the practice of feng Shui was disapproved of and eventually repressed by China during the cultural revolution in the 1960s. However, it has gained popularity in different nations. In recent years, it has witnessed a rise in China as well as Hong Kong also.

In the late 1990s, feng Shui received widespread acceptance throughout all of the Western globe as part of an overall movement which embraced many Eastern or New Age philosophies. Particularly one particular school of feng-shui, referred to as Black Sect Tantric Buddhist Feng Shui (BTB) was able to gain huge popularity. The school was introduced into America United States in the 1980s by Professor Thomas Lin Yun. It was initially a strong link towards Tibetan as well as Chinese Buddhism as well as Taoism and folk wisdom. However, as time has passed, it's gradually modified to fit the Western life style, thereby losing its spiritual roots.

How do they work?

One of the main tenets of fengshui to comprehend is that everything is energy. This means that everything is linked by energy (including your own). The practice of feng-shui brings this energy into harmony to flow positively, that allows you to be successful throughout your life. When there's too much or not enough energy harmony is not achieved.

Yang and yin naturally are in opposition and neither of them can exist without one (similar to darkness and light). Both are in a continuous ever-changing state of flux, and as one grows, the other shrinks. The practice of feng Shui is to find a balance between the ying the yang in your daily life. Furthermore, there needs to be harmony among all five components of Qi (earth as well as water, fire, wood and iron).

Feng Shui requires you to tune in on the frequency and vibrations of the environment. This applies to your indoor and outdoor space, lighting, sounds, smells as well as your furniture arrangement.

When you are tuned into your surroundings, you'll become conscious of your energy and whether or not you're in harmony with the environment around you. It is possible to be feeling out of tune, somewhat "off" in certain areas. According to Feng Shui, this feeling of discomfort is due to an imbalance in energy. To allow harmony to be attained, Qi must be able to flow freely and without restriction by negative energy.

In the present there are numerous feng shui experts mix with the Form as well as the Compass schools and employ them together with the principles of the Yin-Yang theory as well as the theory of the Five Elements. These schools, along with that of Black Sect Tantric Buddhist school are popularly utilized in America and in other Western countries. It is believed that the BTB schools also draw on the Yin-Yang theory and theories of the Five Element. Both are not better or worse than the other, it's a matter of getting the best fit for your and your requirements.

Feng Shui according to The Form as well as the Compass schools requires bagsuas (map of your home or work area) along with a compass in order to determine the best direction for specific reasons. The bagua can be used to determine which elements of a person's life are related to a particular space. The North direction symbolizes your professional career, South - your reputation, East - health and family, West - creativity and children, Northeast - knowledge, Northwest travel, Southeast - wealth, Southwest relationships and love and the central point that connects all eight directions. Each of these areas is additionally associated with a natural element (earth water, fire and wood) or color as well as an animal.

It is believed that the BTB school of feng-shui also employs the bagua, however BTB is focused on the interior of a structure which aligns the bagua to the entryway , not using a Compass. Once the bagua has been correctly placed, you can see which room is linked to which section. For example, if the walls of your home that includes your entryway is in alignment to at the base of your bagua it is associated with any of the three categories that are personal growth as well as your career or direction in life, or blessings. Once you know the space that is connected to a particular aspect in your daily life you are able to use feng shui to bring harmony across your.

There are many ways that you can apply feng shui techniques to enhance your life. Feng shui's principles are applicable to all things from the choice of the place to locate an building, to arrangements for rooms within an apartment and the arrangement of the items at your desk. Harmony is based on the person's requirements, as well as their particular space. For example, if you are looking to boost the creativity of your workplace then you can do some or all of these items: add an eerie wind chime that stimulates the energy of your workspace, put the plants that live around, especially those with white flowers, add circular or oval items, and hang some fun and fun artwork that brings you back to your childhood or you find inspiring.

Another instance is when you're having difficulty sleeping. There are many options to create a tranquil space that can relax and revive you. One of them is to remove electronics like computers and televisions since they can disrupt the energy flow of the space. The opening of windows or using an air purifier to guarantee fresh, oxygenated air is equally important. The bedroom's colors must be warm skin tones, such as chocolate, tan, or cream brown. It should also have soft lighting, such as candlelight (toxic candle-free) and all doors must be shut during your sleep time to let yourself be replenished by the flow of energy in the space.

Chapter 8: The Living Room

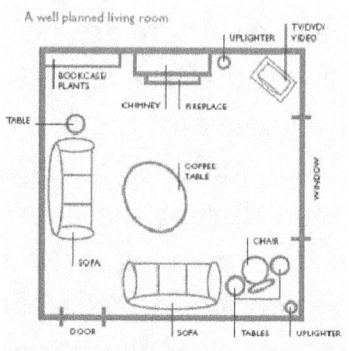

As the living space is the space in the home where you will receive and greet guests, the first thought you should have is to ensure that it's as tidy as you can. This means it has plenty of light sources and the space is clean. What about bringing positivity and energy? What if you could accomplish this by tweaking the furniture arrangement and by adding certain basic elements?

These suggestions are Feng Shui tips that are extremely easy to implement, and extremely efficient:

1. A clock or a timepiece must always be present...

Beyond just telling the time, clocks that are part of Feng Shui have ability to ensure your safety. Experts recommend that you place a wall clock with larger picture frames, with a focus on relatives, mentors and friends. If your clock is equipped with pendulum, set it on the southwest area of your home. not just for its purpose of aesthetics it can ensure your safety while traveling if it is set up in the manner recommended.

2. Beautiful plants

Plants symbolize life and vitality. If you've got one in your living space it will give you more than just fresh air. Set a few plant life in the south part of your living space because it's believed to boost your odds of becoming rich. If you'd like to get known or be recognized for your actions you should put some in the south part of the room. The rich color of plants also indicates healthy health, which is ideal for those who have family members with diseases.

3. Furniture

Since TV draws your attention and diverts you away from what you've set for yourself Experts in Feng Shui recommend that televisions shouldn't be a focal point within the living space. In the event that you can consider buying cabinets that block the television from perspective, or in the event that you do not want to buy one, then place your TV diagonally position.

This can help bring back the focus back to your goals.

4. The Fireplace

Because fireplaces can create warmth in the home they can restore the spark in romance, especially in the event that the marriage or relationship is in trouble. If the fireplace is on the south-facing aspect of the space, it may be a blessing in the realm of wealth and abundance. If it's situated in the northeast you'll likely be more logical and ensure that you make the right choices. This is especially beneficial for those who are still in school.

5. Illustrations

When it comes to photos taking pictures, you need to be very cautious.

Feng Shui experts emphasize the importance of choosing pictures that depict happiness. If the photos you choose are sad or violent, don't put them in the living room. Similar to romance, if you're single, try not using a picture of yourself when you're alone, particularly when you're doing is looking out into space. Abstract art must also be avoided since they can cause chaos to your life.

Family photos that are solid should be enclosed within a metal frame which indicates a sturdy bond. It should be placed on the west-facing wall of the living space. This will bring success.

6. Mirrors

The guidelines for designing with mirrors are easy. The first rule is to not reflect anything that is unappealing, such as garbage piles. In the best way possible place it in a location in which the reflection is a sign of the abundance (food on the table) or the flow or energy (lush plants, or rivers).

Another tip in the case of mirrors: make sure that if they reflect the highest member that the head does not get separated from the body.

The Bedroom

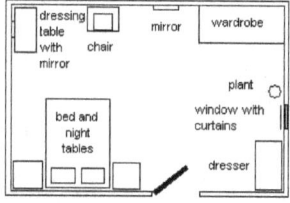

The bedroom is where you can find the most of love and romance. Experts believe that out among all the areas of the home it is the bedroom that is easiest to handle since the methods are easy, straightforward and easy to implement.

1. Ventilation

It is essential to get fresh air in your space, therefore If you have windows, be sure to keep them open frequently. If you have windows that are not working and you want to fix it, invest in a high-quality air purifier. Plants that provide fresh air is not recommended if your bedroom is small. However, in the event that it's big enough, plants should be kept away to the beds.

2. Your love, and your love all by himself.

Check that there's no place in your bedroom that could bring back memories of the past relationship, and ensure that your partner will do the same. This is why experts advise that when you start a family, the bedroom must be completely new so that no trace of love from the past are present.

3. Equality

In terms of the concept of equality Feng Shui professionals suggest that each side of the bed need to be treated equally. It must also be wide enough that when you walk onto it, you do not cross your lover's back. The sides must also be accessible. If you're deciding to fix or choose an existing bed frame, its headboard needs to be strong, indicating that the lovebirds are able to hold on towards each other. If you intend to install bedside lamps be sure both sides are covered.

4. The romantic evening in the city

In the morning, it is best to open your windows wide. At night, they should be a time for sensual lighting, that is to say nothing too bright. This is why it is recommended to use candles, or dim side lighting. The lights will create the tone for the perfect relationship making. The shadows that dim lights cast will provide the attraction of a woman that neither you will be able to resist.

5. Colors and Mirrors

Be cautious when decorating your home with mirrors. As per Feng Shui specialists, it is not recommended to set a mirror the bedroom in front of itthis is because you'll likely draw attention to a third party in your relationship. When it comes to colors, pick the ones that are soothing and, simultaneously, appealing. The color spectrum varies between light brown and pink. Do not make red the predominant color, but you could add a few touches throughout the space.

6. Photos

In terms of images, ensure that the primary photos that show up are that you with your partner. In addition, adding photos of the entire family can be distracting and only compromise the privacy that you are creating.

7. The Buzz

The most important rule to follow in design of your bedroom is to Never put anything in your bedroom that could keep you from resting, sleeping and falling in love. This is everything from workout equipment papers, to household bills! These suggestions also work for Feng Shui! Therefore, if you wish for that your room to turn into one that is a place where romance blossoms and sparks is ignited, get rid of any distractions!

The Kitchen

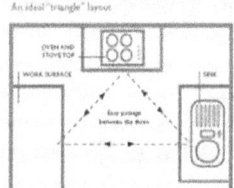

The days of kitchens were the only exception from style. In the past, in our history kitchens had to be neat (because it is where food items are cooked) However, they didn't have to be planned, and even more, and styled in accordance with Feng Shui. This isn't the norm today. If you're looking to create an Feng Shui perfect kitchen, that can enhance the lives of your family members Follow these tips:

1. Stand your ground

If you're thinking of seriously remodel your kitchen in order to make your kitchen Feng Shui perfect, make sure you have earthen objects like potteries. If not, you should think about changing your countertops to neutral colors. As per experts earthy elements or neutral colors will keep you alert-- which is a necessity when handling hazardous substances like fire and knives.

2. Concerning the gadgets

Smaller homes often transform their kitchen into a dining roomexperts are not against it, but they have their own opinions regarding adding gadgets to the dining and kitchen.

The Feng Shui theory is that the TV, or any other electronic device you have that can distract you is not to be used while you are spending time cooking or eating. It's not only because you're disobeying the blessings, however, it is more about distracting the communications that needs to be present in the family.

As much as you can take away these distractions, or, if your space isn't able to accommodate it, turn it off while you prepare your meal and eating.

3. The splendor of the chef

Feng Shui also suggests that your kitchen should always have an enthusiastic and confident cook. This doesn't mean you have to buy a statue of something, but it is important to ensure that the cook at home (more typically, the mom) is happy and confident when cooking food for the family.

To ensure that she is happy Keep the space for cooking on the kitchen island. This will ensure that the cook will feel that she's an integral part within the home. In order for her to feel confident it is essential to be aware of the world around her when she cooks and that's why she should be in front of the front door or window.

If this isn't the layout of your kitchen (meaning the cook's back faces towards the door) You can make a compromise the look of your kitchen by installing mirrors. It is also helpful when the stove is in good operating good condition.

4. Safety first

Knives should be kept away from places where they can be easily accessed by anyone. Fens shui experts say that the reason it is best to keep them out of sight isn't just for security but also because of the sense of security they provide. When a cook comes across many sharp objects that are hung on the walls of the kitchen she's likely to be irritable and stressed. If that's the case when she cooks, the food she makes for everyone in the family will not be as appealing and enthusiasm.

5. Doubling the fortune and wealth

According to Feng Shui, burners of the stove represent wealth and fortune. by doubling their numbers, you will increase your wealth and fortune. A simple mirror can help. Simply place the mirror above the burners, or over the stove's hood. ensure that the burners are reflecting onto the mirror. If you can see eight stoves instead of four, then you've come up with the perfect solution.

6. Leaky faucets

As we mentioned previously that the kitchen is the space in the home in which the entire family is fed and the energy is flowing. This means that it is connected to do with not only the health and wealth and physical health, but also the emotional.

If your faucets continue to leaky, make sure to fix them immediately. Feng Shui experts emphasize that leaks draw away not only money from the family, but the energy of your entire family.

7. Space is added

Because the kitchen is the heart of health and wealth, making it large is a wise choice. This can be the most difficult issue for those living in an apartment with a limited space. However, don't be concerned experts say that you could compensate by creating the illusion of having a larger area. By installing mirrors in your doorways and making the kitchen as clean as is possible are two most effective ways to add more the space in your kitchen.

8. Revitalize

Reviving your kitchen is simple. All you need to do is ensure there are plants and flowers around the room or, if you can't afford them just add some fresh fruit on the kitchen table or on the countertops.

It is essential to cook delicious meals by cooking at the least two times each week. Because of busy agendas, the only things the family members can handle now is fast meals and eating in a hurry. According to Feng Shui, families should cook in their kitchens with passion at least two times a week. This means that the food you prepare should be elaborate with lots of details and also delicious.

The Bathroom

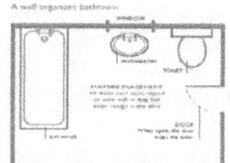

Bathrooms are a space where the privacy of the individual is at its best. Some homeowners do not take the time to organize their bathrooms since they is the sole ones who use the bathroom. The only exception can be made when visitors are scheduled to show up. But, Feng Shui experts reiterate that you should pay attention to the bathroom as it is usually the most unlucky spot in the home. The reason for this is that the water drains constantly out of the tub and toilet.

The least fortunate position for bathrooms is to be in the north or the south, since these are the regions that are rich and romantic. A bathroom located in those regions means that money and love will be flushed out or eliminated. However, in reality the bathroom you have is an unlucky location regardless of its location. It makes the Feng Shui method more important.

Relax. This doesn't mean that when your bathroom is in the two positions above it is a sure thing that you'll be there for the rest of your life. You can mitigate the negative consequences by using the methods in the following article.

1. The sound of chimes is soothing.

If your bathroom is on the north or southwest part of your home, it is essential to install wind chimes made of metal within the space. This is to eliminate negative energy. Feng Shui specialists also suggested to purchase the wind chime, it should no Chinese symbol. The purpose of the chime is that it helps get rid of bad energies, and not activate it, hence there are no symbols.

2. Crystals

If your bathroom is situated in the south part of the house, you can get rid of negative energies by placing crystals inside the windows. The crystals will absorb negative energy, so that your family will be safe.

The main issue in this method is the cleaning from the stones. Since they absorb a significant amount of the negative energy that is a part of the house It is recommended that they be cleaned regularly. It is possible to cleanse them each month or every week and utilize methods like moonlighting or the burying of the crystals (the crystals) beneath the ground or under herbs.

3. Plants

If the bathroom is located to the north of your home It is possible to eliminate negative energy by putting plants next to the window. This will not only improve the quality of the air you breathe, it will also lift your spirit.

4. Lamps and candles

If the bathroom is on the east part of your house It is a great option to put candles or even glitter lamps in the bathroom. The heat from these items will help dispel the negative energy. In addition it can also provide an ambiance that is romantic and will help soothe the mood of a person who is unhappy.

5. If your toilet is located above your kitchen, bedroom or the main door

Feng Shui experts suggest that having a bathroom directly above the kitchen, bedroom or the main entrance is unfortunate. It is possible to avoid the luck by turning the light off in your bathroom 3 hours every day.

6. Water that is stagnant

The water in the bathroom and toilet is constantly being flushed out or drained It is essential to counter this by placing water inside an Urn. This will ensure that the energy and luck will remain throughout the flushing and draining.

Note: The items that we have listed above should not be put in any place any other than in the location that we have specified. Examples: don't place crystals in your bathroom if it is located in the north part of your house or place plants in bathrooms that are located in the southern part of the home.

7. If you are using the bathroom, ensure that the doors unlocked

However... take care to be cautious. If the bathroom is in close proximity to the kitchen or in the bedroom , where beds can be seen or if the bathroom is also facing the other entrance... ensure that you close the door while you bathe. In other cases, experts recommend that you bathe by opening the doors (not always, particularly if you have children or guests in the vicinity).

The Home Office

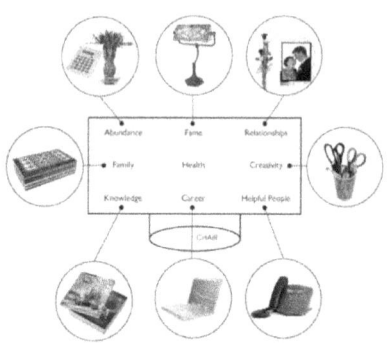

The office in your home is where the majority of your ideas will be developed. It is essential to ensure that the space in your home can be Feng Shui perfect.

1. The place

In contrast to other areas of the home The home office is extremely adaptable in terms of place. When you set it up, be sure that it's not located in the bedroom as it could disrupt sleeping and romantic. If you're in the midst of a tiny space and are unable to put the office in your bedroom, ensure that you have a partition, such as a wood screen or partition.

Do not put the office under the stairs as the space can get crowded and may hinder formulation. The ideal location for a home office would be one with a ceiling that is high that symbolizes high accomplishments for career and business.

2. The power desk

The desk should be brand new , so as not to mix concepts of your previous owners with the ones of you. The desk should also be constructed out of wood, as glass desks are susceptible to breaking and may be the symbol of commercial deals and promotions to break too. Be sure to choose a sturdy table not one with there are any components missing. To ensure that you are heading on the right path it is suggested to keep nothing under your table, particularly trash bins.

3. Your position

For your location ensure that you're facing the doors (although they are not exactly in a direct manner) and your eyes may be able to cover the window. If you are facing the door, the Feng Shui theory has it that there are lots happening in your back-- not ideal for any type of job or career. The door is facing you and looking out the windows gives you an advantage in the tactical arena.

In terms of support and stability, be sure your back is in a solid wall, not the window.

4. Symbolisms

In terms of decor and style It is recommended to put up images or quotes that represent what you would like to achieve in your life. Photos of your family members are great because they serve as a support system, however, you should not include too many of them as they could create distractions.

5. Separating your personal and professional life

In addition to ensuring that your office space is as remote as you can from your bedroom, you should also be sure to take the necessary steps to keep it from your daily life. It is possible to do this by locking the door every time you visit or by making the proper plan. Rituals are also beneficial as the ritual can prepare you and signal to your brain that business is returning. One example of a great business routine is to burn a candle or to play some music prior to working.

This doesn't mean that you can't "include" your personal characteristics into the workplace. Experts advise people to build their office according to their personal style and character in order to boost security and comfort. In the end, it is impossible to think clearly if the space that he's currently in isn't his own.

Chapter 9: Understanding Feng Shui

Before proceeding with the steps to create the perfect Feng Shui living room, first you must understand the fundamental principles that are the basis of Feng Shui. This is a brief introduction.

What is Feng Shui?

Feng Shui can be described as harmonizing the energy fields produced by objects around you so that the total energy (Chi) can empower you to achieve success in all your endeavors.

There are 5 Feng Shui elements:

1. Metal – This element enhances a person's inventiveness and good planning skills.

2. Water – This element indicates a person's interest in the arts. It also signifies that the person has great insight and good leadership abilities.

3. Fire – This element is indicative of a person who is highly energetic.

4. Wood – This element indicates that the person has the ability to be a good team player. It also indicates new beginnings, growth and development.

5. Earth – This element indicates that the person has good control over his emotions. It also signifies nourishment and stability.

There are colors related to each element. You can use these colors to enhance your Chi or energy. Furthermore, use your personal element in congruence with your colors to determine good Feng Shui enhancements.

The colors that correspond to your elements are the following:

1. Metal – gray and white

2. Water – black and blue

3. Fire – red, yellow, orange, purple, and pink

4. Wood – brown and green

5. Earth – earthly colors such as light brown, sandy, and pink

In addition, Feng Shui uses two types of Bagua energy maps in determining auspicious locations for smooth energy flow.

Two types of Bagua Energy Maps

1. Compass Bagua map

2. Form Bagua Map

You can use EITHER of the two maps, it's really your choice depending on which one works best for you and your home. The key to choosing which map to use really is through a small amount of pre-planning with each map, then determine which suits you best. Most people find the Form map better for smaller room-by-room projects, but if the Compass map works well for you, then go for it!

Compass Bagua map – This Feng Shui map is more commonly used when addressing an entire house or building, rather than in the decoration of one particular room. It's composed of 8 sections with a center space, and you'll need to use a compass to align it with your house.

Compass Map Example

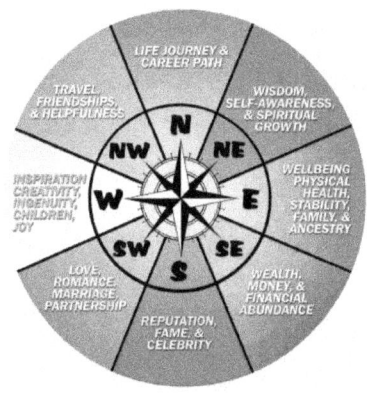

Enhance the flow of energy anywhere by arranging the area according to this map. Use a compass device to pinpoint the correct orientation. Place items relating to your element and colors in the most auspicious locations to ensure that an unimpeded flow of good energy occurs.

This map can also help you in locating your best command position through your personal Kua number. Your command position is the place where you can view the entire area and be able to watch who comes in and out of your living room.

Your Kua numbers are computed based on your year of birth and gender. They can be used in charting your elements and the colors that you can use to enhance your Chi. In summary, this Kua number can prove useful for enhancing your good Feng Shui.

Steps in computing your Kua numbers

Step #1 - Obtain the last two digits of your birth year. Add them to produce a whole number.

Example: Birth year is 1965

6 + 5 = 11, since the answer is a two digit number, add them again until you get a one-digit number.

1+1 = 2

Step #2 – If you're male, subtract the above answer from 10

Based on the computation above, the answer is 2

Hence, 10 – 2 = 8, so 8 is your personal Kua number

Step #3 – If you're female, add the answer to 5.

Based on the computation in step #1, the answer is 2

So, 2 + 5 = 7, so 7 is your personal Kua number.

Using your Kua Number:

Based on the computations above, your Kua number is 7. Using your Kua number, locate your most lucky space on the Lo-Shu square below:

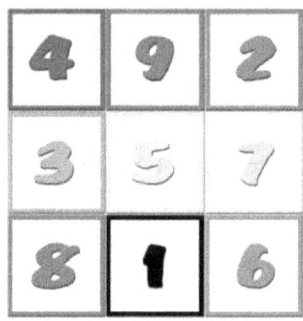

Based on this "magic" square, you can determine your lucky position. Your Kua number location is the best area for you. For the example above, 8 (male) and 7 (female) are the Kua numbers. These are the bottom row, first left square, and the middle row, last right square. This method applies with the other Kua numbers too. The colors are: For 8 – blue and for 7 – pastel or light colors.

You could also interpret your Kua numbers this way, in terms of which way you should face:

Kua numbers for the east group = 1, 3, 4, 9

Kua numbers for the west group = 2, 5, 6, 7, 8

The east group involves locations facing the east, or southeast, or the north or south areas, meaning you'll be best positioned when facing these directions.

The west group includes locations facing the west, southwest and northwest.

Now, you have to take advantage of these positions to enhance the power of your good Feng Shui. Let's say, for example, you're in the east group. That means to attain the best "command" position in your living room, you'll want to position the sofa to face east, if possible. If other family members' kua numbers are different, consider positioning the furniture in a way such that everyone can sit facing their best position. This is not a requirement, but rather considered to be an "optimization," so don't worry if it doesn't work out perfectly.

Form Bagua Map Example

Your Form Bagua Map is similar to your Compass Bagua Map but instead of orienting it using a compass, it's aligned with your home according to whichever wall on which the entry door is located.

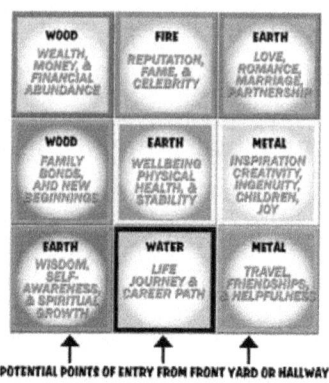

POTENTIAL POINTS OF ENTRY FROM FRONT YARD OR HALLWAY

By using this Form Map, you can enhance any area or space using the descriptions. Align your door with the entry point and start enhancing the energy force accordingly.

For example, if your living room is located smack in the middle of your home, then it's located in the "Wellbeing, Physical Health, and Stability" square, and the governing element is "Earth." But if the living room is on the opposite side of the house as the front entry door, at the far left-hand corner (reading the map with your back against the entry door), then it's located in the "Wealth, Money, and Financial Abundance" square, and "Wood" is the governing element. Get the idea?

Chapter 10: Guide To Feng Shui Living Room Decor

Designing your living room to enhance your Feng Shui is an excellent idea. You have the right to use any and all means at your disposal to attain success in every area of your life.

The living room plays a major role in the smooth flow of Chi in your surroundings because many momentous activities happen in your living room. It's where you receive guests. It's where you gather around with family members and friends during holidays and events. It's where you conduct some of your business transactions. Thus, maximizing the Chi in your living room is good Feng Shui practice.

To do this, here's a guide you can employ:

Dos

- Do use decor that has warm colors based on your living room's location in the Bagua Map.

- Do use inspiring images and photos.

- Do use happy family pictures.

- Do use décor with the 5 elements, but focus on your element.

- Do use crystal decor that can help harmonize energy forces.

- Do ensure that colors of each decoration are in harmony with the other decoration's colors and with the color of the entire room.

- Do use metal frames for family pictures to ensure good luck.

Don'ts

- Don't use violent images.

- Don't position decorations with unharmonious elements close together, such as, fire and water.

- Don't use objects with sharp edges or corners.

- Don't use L-shaped decorations because they resemble destructive arrows.

- Don't decorate your walls with sad and depressing paintings or images.

- Don't use loud and offensive colors.

- Don't place decorations where their edges point directly at the sofas.

Observing these dos and don'ts will ensure that your living room is enhanced using good Feng Shui. In instances like this, the Chi becomes one powerful force of energy that can boost your own energy towards success.

Chapter 11: Proper Feng Shui Living Room Layout

The layout of your living room must conform to good Feng Shui organization principles to allow energy to flow freely around the room. The most important thing that you ought to remember is that every room in your home has to be clean, free from clutter, well-ventilated, and well-lighted to promote the smooth and harmonious flow of the different energy fields inside each room. Only then can you enhance the Feng Shui in your home.

Here is an example of how to arrange the layout of your living room:

1. Major furniture or sofa

The major piece of furniture must be placed in a command position. This is usually your sofa. From where you are seated, you have to be able to observe the entire room. It has to be facing towards the door and not facing away from the door. Ideally, this will correspond with your Kua number position, although it isn't absolutely necessary.

There should be no sharp objects including the sharp edges of tables or other structures pointing at you in your command position.

If there are several sofas, they must be arranged in a circular manner to prevent disruption of the Chi. This arrangement will allow optimum interaction between the groups, enhancing the Feng Shui Chi inside the room.

Avoid positioning your sofa directly below a window. It should also be supported by a firm wall or structure.

For solitary chairs, you can balance the Feng Shui energy by adding a small side-table, or by placing another chair in the room.

Placing your sofa under a beam is bad Feng Shui as well. Notice that hazardous and unsafe positions are categorized as bad Feng Shui.

1. Television sets

Position TV sets in a corner or at the side of a room, not in the center. This applies to any of your musical equipment as well, including stereos and radios.

You can build a sturdy cabinet where your TV can be stored out of sight, when not in use. If this is not possible, you can also place a glass panel in front of your TV, so you can use this as a mirror – when your TV is not in use – to reflect good spots in your living room and bounce the energy back from them.

2. Stereo Equipment

Electronic type equipment must not occupy the primary spot in your living room. They shouldn't be the focus of attention when you enter your living room. They can be placed in a well-lighted corner.

3. Cabinets

Cabinets can be placed in a corner where their weight is supported by a firm, strong wall. Wooden cabinets are preferred and are good Feng Shui materials. You can use metal or steel cabinets if your element is metal. Just balance the Yin (negative) and the Yang (positive) through addition of other wooden objects.

4. Mirrors

Mirrors are good Feng Shui in your living room. They make the room appear spacious and can reflect positive energy. The mirror has to be positioned in a place where it reflects the most vibrant part of your living room. It must not be facing the dining table.

Avoid placing your mirror in a position where you can see yourself when you're standing by a window, but position it in such a way that it can reflect anyone entering your main door. Never place mirrors in the south area of a room. Place it in an area where it can reflect the most comfortable and beautiful spot in your living room.

5. Clocks

A clock in the living room is good Feng Shui. It should not be placed near your dining table. An antique grandfather's clock can be a superb centerpiece of art in your living room.

Circular clocks are preferable to square ones because they enhance the flow of energy more effectively. Square clocks can also be a source of bad Chi or bad energy.

6. Aquariums

An aquarium can bring abundance and good luck to your home. Placing a square or rectangular aquarium in the southeast area of your room, or a round shaped aquarium in the north area of your living room will boost your financial and career success. Don't place them in the west, northwest or south areas because any water-related objects placed in these areas produce negative Feng Shui energy.

7. Fireplace

Constructing a fireplace is one way of enhancing your Chi. It enhances the energy for success in your career and education. It bolsters your chances of a long lasting romance and success in relationships. You can position the fireplace in the south, southwest, or northeast areas of your living room.

8. Lighting fixtures

There must be a light bulb in all areas of your living room. Avoid dark corners in a room that is supposed to be the liveliest and brightest area in your home. Avoid furniture that can cover the light coming from your lighting fixtures. They're obstructing the positive Feng Shui energy.

9. Plants

Plants are great Feng Shui items because they bring positive energy into any space. Scientifically, they also promote health by taking in the carbon dioxide that you exhale, and giving back clean oxygen that you can inhale.

Their best positions are in the east, southeast, and south areas of your living room.

For health purposes, prevent the accumulation of water in your plants because this is an ideal breeding place for mosquitoes and bugs. You can acquire Dengue fever or H-fever through mosquitoes.

10. Wall Decor

You can display beautiful pictures in the west or south areas of your living room. Use images that depict joy or success such as a smiling woman cuddling her son, or a beautiful sunrise. You can also adorn the wall with a happy family picture that brings back good memories.

These are some of the furniture arrangements and decorations that you can use to harmonize the energy in your living room. Imagine the Chi energy as water flowing into the room. Are there any obstacles that can obstruct its flow? These are also the obstructions for your good Feng Shui energy.

Chapter 12: Steps In Good Living Room Feng Shui

Using an organized system in implementing your Feng Shui will prevent a waste of time and energy. It will also facilitate the process and ensure that no errors are committed. To assist you in utilizing good Feng Shui in your living room, here are some reliable steps you should follow.

Step #1 – Prepare a plan to clean up and de-clutter your living room

Prepare a detailed plan on how to clean up and de-clutter your living room by specifying what items to dispose of and what items to keep. Also specify where you'll be placing the items that you would like to keep. Do you place them in the garage temporarily? Or will you put them in a corner of the dining room? Every detail must be ironed out, and waiting to be implemented.

What about the items you plan to dispose of? Will you donate them to charity or will you throw them directly into the garbage? You should write down the details, so you won't spend time deciding where to place the items.

Step #2 – Prepare a layout plan for your living room

How do you intend to arrange the furniture in your living room? Measure the furniture and the spaces you plan to place them in to see if they fit together. If you're buying new furniture, ensure that proper measurements are taken so it will fit properly in the room. Your plan should mark the various areas of the room with the furniture that you intend to place in that particular space. This step can be interchangeable with step #3. Do whatever suits you better.

Step #3 – Clean up and de-clutter the area

Clean the entire area thoroughly and discard all clutter. A dirty, cluttered area circulates bad energy and bad luck. Be organized and stick to the plan that you have prepared.

Be sure you properly clean the ceiling, walls, and floor of your living room before proceeding to step #4.

Step #4 – Install proper lighting fixtures

The room should be well-lighted; there must be no dark areas. Your living room needs bright lights to promote the smooth and harmonious flow of energy. Always maintain proper lighting and be sure to fix broken or dead bulbs promptly. In corners where there's no light, you can use bright colors to increase illumination of that area. Similarly, mirrors that reflect light from a different spot in your living room are good options.

Step #5 – Allow proper ventilation

For good Feng Shui, the living room ought to be properly ventilated. Air has to flow freely to ensure those in the living room are breathing well.

Step #6 – Arrange the furniture

You can now arrange the furniture as specified above for good Feng Shui. If you're not sure about other items, use your intuition and good sense. Is the position of the item in congruence with the other items in the room? Is its location safe? Is it visually balanced and pleasant to view? For instance, it's not wise to place a fountain close to electronic equipment, nor is it good to position your bicycle near your TV set.

Good Feng Shui involves observance of health and safety practices. Sometimes, all you have to do is arrange your furniture properly to prevent hazardous situations and disease.

Step #7 – Enhance the good Feng Shui of your living room through its decor

Enhance your good Feng Shui by decorating the room with recommended Feng Shui items including: bright and joyful images, happy family pictures, and inspiring landscapes and images. Decorate the room with your designated colors and elements based on your Bagua Map or Kua numbers.

If your living room's location is at the south and southwest portion of your Bagua energy map, the elements involved are fire and earth. The colors involved are red, yellow, orange, purple and pink for fire, and earthly colors such as light brown, sandy and pink. The colors will depend on your living room's location.

Bring in items that can brighten your living room and display your personality. Gold and silver trophies are good examples. But, take note not to clutter the room as a crowded living room prevents positive energy from circulating well.

Step #8 – Maintain the good Feng Shui of your living room

You have to maintain the smooth flow of energy in the room. Dispose of your clutter daily and clean up your mess promptly after each activity. Experiment with your colors and elements and observe what works best for you.

To make your living room more personalized, you're allowed to use your own personal designs. Everything inside your living room must complement each other. This includes the colors of your walls, wall paper, decorations, and furniture.

Needless to say, every item must produce energy that brings out the best in you and your family members.

Chapter 13: Best Feng Shui Living Room Colors

The colors of your living room must blend with each other. If you want to use your Feng Shui colors, then refer to your Bagua Map and to your Lo-Shu square. As discussed in Chapter 1, there are colors indicated for each element. You can decide the shade of color based on your element and preference, but brighter and lighter shades are usually recommended.

As presented in Chapter 1, the following colors correspond to these elements:

• Gray and white – If your element is metal. The gray and white colors represent children, joy, future, travel, and helpful friends in the Bagua Map.

• Black and blue – If your element is water. Black and blue colors denote knowledge and cultivation, career and self-journey.

- Red, yellow, orange, purple and pink – If your element is fire. These colors indicate fame, reputation, and health.

- Brown and green – If your element is wood. Brown and green denote wealth, prosperity, new beginnings, and family.

- Earthly colors, light brown, sandy and pink – If your element is earth. These colors also denote health, marriage, and relationships.

Here are some good color combinations:

- Neutral earthly tones

- Shades of gray, brown, light yellow

- Navy blue and gray

- Pale blue and white

- Mustard yellow, apple green, and brown hues

- Rosy pink, white, and light red

- Light blue, dirty white, and antique gray

- Gray and creamy white
- Apple green and yellow

Pale colors create a spacious ambiance, while dark colors will make the room seem smaller.

Of course, you can rely on your personal preferences and taste and let the colors reflect your personality but you should nevertheless incorporate the Feng Shui recommendations to get the best results.

Aside from using your Feng Shui colors, the rule of thumb in using colors for the living room is to blend colors that complement each other to result in a living room that is welcoming, comfortable, and uplifting.

At a glance, a person entering the living room should feel the warmth of the people living in the house.

You can also hire an expert designer to help you decide on colors for your living room. The most important thing is to create an atmosphere where colors allow you to interact fruitfully with the other people. The resulting ambiance must be one of comfort, vitality, and joy.

After all, good Feng Shui denotes good vibes that are in congruence and unity with all objects around you.

Chapter 14: Tips On Proper Living Room Feng Shui

Feng Shui encompasses a string of principles and beliefs. As you practice it, you'll learn how to incorporate other information harmoniously into your act. It's a continuous process that has to be developed and enhanced all the time. Don't be afraid to make mistakes as long as you learn from them. Perceive them as your stepping stones on your road to success and self-fulfillment.

This list includes significant tips that you can apply for your living room Feng Shui.

1. Cleanliness is a must for good Feng Shui. Foremost, the area must be clean. Good Feng Shui can never happen in unclean surroundings, so tidy up.

2. Clutter is bad Feng Shui. Always de-clutter your room, no matter how busy you are. This is to avoid accumulation of unwanted items that can disrupt the flow of positive Chi (total energy).

3.   Well-ventilated rooms elicit good Feng Shui. Free flowing air balances the Yin (negative) and Yang (positive) energies. This will yield a Chi that can eradicate bad luck and can bring in good fortune.

4.   Proper lightning must be observed in each room. Each of your rooms has special lighting requirements. Be aware of them. For your living room, bright lights promote good Feng Shui.

5.   An organized living room is good Feng Shui. This applies to all the rooms in your house. Ask help from all your family members to organize their own stuff, so that positive energy can flow effortlessly. When each family member organizes and cleans his space, it will harmonize all your energy forces to unify into one powerful force that can attract success.

6.   Express your style in your living room design. Good Feng Shui can go hand in hand with your own personal design. Be ingenious to find ways to do this. Your living room is where you do most of your

activities with your family so, it ought to be designed brilliantly.

7. Good Feng Shui will make you comfortable and secure. If you feel unease after making all your Feng Shui arrangements, then something must be wrong.

8. Good Feng Shui need not be expensive. To save on cost, choose your materials wisely by considering durability and affordability. There are thousands of items that are durable and, at the same time, inexpensive. You'll just have to be patient and search both online and offline.

9. If you have a pet, the living room is not the best place for his primary "spot" or bed. You can choose a small corner near your bathroom or construct a pet house for him in your front yard.

10. Your living room should radiate harmonious relationships between family members. If it doesn't, that's bad Feng Shui for you. Even if your relationships aren't perfect, accomplish the

recommendations for good Feng Shui, and gradually, you'll notice improvements.

11. For the best Feng Shui, you need all 5 elements in your living room. Just ascertain that each is located in its appropriate space. Use your Bagua energy maps to determine this.

12. Your front door plays a major role in Feng Shui. Your front door usually leads to your living room, so don't put any obstructions in the path to your front door. Also, it should not be directly opposite another door, especially an exit door, to prevent energy flowing directly out of your home.

13. Avoid adorning your living room with plants that have sharp leaves. They're sha chi's, which are sharp items pointing at you. This is bad Feng Shui.

14. Your living room must be able to accommodate all members of your family. There should be a space allotted to each member so that you can gather all together if needed.

15. Electronic equipment such as TVs should be properly hidden. They shouldn't occupy the primary spot in your living room. You can "hide" them by covering them when not in use.

16. Avoid overcrowding your living room. Each decoration must complement the other items inside the room. Too much of anything will obstruct good Feng Shui energy.

17. Appropriate colors can help heal and energize your mind and body. When you choose your proper Feng Shui colors, they can revitalize your energy and keep you healthy.

18. Furniture that has rounded ends is preferable. Sharp edges and corners can bring bad Feng Shui because these are considered energy sha Chi's that attack you, instead of empowering you.

19. The fireplace can be the center of your living room. This is ideal because family members can gather around it and interact. The flow of positive energy fields

will be smooth and in harmony with each other.

20. Chi (total positive energy) must be able to flow freely. It should flow around the living room without any obstructions. This will harmonize all energy forces into one powerful Chi.

21. Your living room should be welcoming and comfortable. It must project an atmosphere of warmth and happiness. This will enhance your Chi.

22. Mirrors are essential in the living room. Position strategically, to optimize their positive energy.

23. Continue Feng Shui in other rooms in your house. After implementing Feng Shui recommendations in your room, you can proceed to other rooms in your house.

24. Avoid placing water based equipment improperly. It shouldn't be placed in the south, west, or northwest areas of your living room. This is bad Feng Shui.

25. Maximize the use of your Bagua energy maps. This is because they're essential tools for you to achieve good Feng Shui. They're applicable in any area or space around you.

26. An image or photo of a horse or galloping horse is good Feng Shui. It must be placed in the south area of your living room as good Feng Shui for your recognition and fame.

27. A fountain of water in the middle of the living space can emit positive Chi. It can be placed in the north to help you advance your career and the achievement you desire.

28. A table in the living room that's neat and tidy emits positive energy. It's a vital resource of energy that is positive, don't forget about it.

29. You must ensure a smooth and steady stream of power. You can achieve this by removing objects that could block the flow of energy.

30. Encourage family members to learn the art of Feng Shui. You can identify the Bagua energy zones and personal Kua numbers for your family members, and then synchronize these, so that your energies are in sync and harmony with one the other. This creates a powerful power source for positive energies for your home.

These are all great tips for practicing Feng Shui. Implementing every one of the Feng Shui recommendations will help you to achieve success at work, your home as well as in relationships.

Chapter 15: Top 28 Wealth Feng Shui Tips For Your Home!

Be sure to pay attention to each wealth-related area of your home right now. Begin with the area you spend most of your time in, or at your home office. (Or the place where you're earning money if you work at your home.) Also, make sure you clean up and recharge every Abundance zone within your home.

1. The first thing to do is to tidy, clean and tidy. It's not a lot of fun but think that you will be blessed when you clean up and arrange. This is a simple way to get the blood flowing and will give your wealth corner an air of freshness and a new beginning by cleaning. Awesome!

2. At this point it is essential to eliminate things that are no longer useful to you broken items, broken furniture and unneeded clutter in the home. This could take a longer. If you've been accumulating the mess in your home for five years, it is time to spend some time to clear it. Every

thing in your home needs to be in its own place where it is. The more space Chi or energy has to circulate and flow, the better for your financial health. Find some boxes, label them donate to, keep, sell or garbage, and start organizing them.

3. As you tidy, up, set a figure you'd like to boost your income by, it's just in your head at this point. (Don't be concerned about way the Abundance will appear in the future; we'll talk about it later.)Think about the ways you'll spend, save or pamper yourself when you have the money. I'll get into setting goals later.

4. Make Your Personal Prosperity Jar. It sounds wonderful does it not? Well, I'll tell ya, it works......directions will be right below this list.

5 I know it sounds odd, but put your lids on your toilets. For Feng Shui the lid up could represent all your wealth that is flushed down the toilet.

6 The front entrance itself should be super Duper super clean. Your front entrance is

at the center from which all of the power enters your home. Check that it's in good shape and tidy. An extra coat is never a bad thing neither! It's always a good luck color.

7 - In front of the door,, make sure that it's clean and swept. A lovely potted plant the other the front or back of your door will bring good Chi and harmony.

8. On the inside of the front doors, be sure that all clutter is taken away. Shoes should be put away in a drawer in a closet or in the closet.

9 The most popular colors for the wealth corner are red, purple as well as bright yellow and green. Pick the one you find yourself drawn to in the moment and then include a splash. For instance, put up an art piece in red work as well as purple throw cushions, or some yellow/gold candles.

10 Place anything you believe as "lucky" within the wealth Corner. The most lucky objects that are part of Feng Shui are gold

coins, (you can use any coins you want) gemstones, crystals, and anything which is symbolic of wealth for you.

11 ~ Clean your kitchen inside out! It is the place where you feed yourself, and it is essential to kept clean and clutter-free. Clear out your Tupperware area, clean out the cupboards, wash the refrigerator.

12 Repair or eliminate any broken items. It's time! Let the item go. I'm sure it's been laying around for two years or longer. (You are aware of the items I'm talking about.) Donate it to your local charity. clothes or appliances are always appreciated. You can also give it to your friend, sell items you don't use anymore. Make sure to dispose of everything in a proper way. When you have completed this step, you'll feel more relaxed and confident in moving forward.

13 - Add beautiful flowers for your office or living area. The flowers bring life to the area and will brighten up every day.

14 Place an effigy in your wealth corner. I love a tea light. If I light it each day, I think about the happiness that has come into my life so far. Be extra cautious around burning flames.

15 Goldfish represent the symbol of Luck and luck. Consider having one in your living space. (In the wealth zone) It's always good to keep an animal companion!

16 Place Lucky Bamboo or any other plant with rounded leaves around your Wealth Corner. I set my own in a vase with water. Make sure the vase is kept clear and clean. It should also have clean water. Be wary of Catus as well as sharp-spiked plants within your Abundance space.

17 If your area is dark, place an electric lamp in the corner! The nightlight, as you are familiar with for children, is recommended to keep in place when you can. It will shine continuously on your Prosperity , increasing the energy level and making the "pathway" easily to find you.

18 ~ Keep your bathroom door shut. If you leave the door open, it could suck away the chi from areas that are vitally important like the wealth. We do not want this!

19 Create an attractive fountain that flows with fresh water. It is a symbol of water, as well. In Feng Shui water represents the flow of wealth. Make sure to keep this spotless throughout the day. It is not recommended for bedrooms.

20 Find some pictures of gold or other symbols of prosperity and set them as wallpaper for your mobile phone to make sure you look at it every day. The things you pay attention to grow!

21 Create the Vision Board in your office make sure to focus your vision board to your business (if you're an entrepreneurial type) or wealth, money, prosperity and abundance. Instructions below.

22. Keep sharp objects from the zone. Scissors and other sharp objects could be a

sign of sharp end or the cutting off of cords or nerves, etc.

23 Hang a wood or bamboo wind-chime. This will bring luck as the Wealth Corner's ingredient is Wood. This can also block energy from entering the window if there's an opening in this space. It also neutralizes negative energies and creates a tranquil space that is always clean.

24 ~ Wash dishes right away. Do not put dishes in the sink, especially when you're out to earn money.

25. Take receipts from your wallet! They will be there for a long time! If you are keeping receipts for work, use an accordion-like folder, like an recipe envelope, in the tabs that are appropriate. In addition to keeping them out of your wallet, but they're more organized as well! If you store your invoices inside your wallet, it is a reminder that you will always have to pay bills.

26 Here's some more to clean ....the fridge and stove should be sparkling both inside and outside!

27 - Throw away old food! This can lead to stale and energy that is not as appealing and can contaminate fresh food as well! (Please compost)

28 Your wallet must be in good condition. If it's deteriorating, this symbolizes your financial status not in good condition. The best colors for wallets include gold, but you can also go for flashy red, black, and brown. (Brown keeps you focused on the spending habits you make.)

Implementing these strategies does not require breaking the bank for new purchases also. This is the scenario we're trying to avoid. Time to be creative here. Repurpose things you haven't used for an extended period of time, or use place mats to bring the color to a table. Most items can buy at a discount shop for a minimal price. Find a friend who's skilled with plants to cut and cultivate a part of their garden, and especially one with good financial resources so that you can get some of their energy and take that rich and good feeling they bring.

Your items don't have to be traditional oriental objects and you can choose what is meaningful to you. If you think a Chinese fortunate cat seems like something you are looking for, take it to heart However, please remember that it's mostly about the sensation that a luck brings to you and more than the actual "it" is.

Chapter 16: How To Make Your Own Prosperity Jar! !

It's easy...OK take the jar with an elongated mouth, rather than a the base and a lid. Always ensure that the jar is spotless.

Include anything that you think is fortunate in the jar, along with your precious stones. Some good things to include these include coins made of gold and coins of all types pictures of luck and an object, or photo from the moment when you felt lucky and that money came into.

I designed two Prosperity Jars and set them side-by-side in my Abundance space in order to can manifest wealth through partnership. This is the main ingredient to growing your company!

Next , I cut pieces of fabric that have blue, brown, red metallic, and green. They represent all the colors/elements of the Feng Shui map. Then I cut tiny squares in each of the colors, and then place them inside. Typically, you're supposed to put the fabric and then place it on top of the lid however I was a designer in the past and it looks better inside the container. If you decide to place your fabric to the outside , then put the same five colors of thread or string and tie the fabric on top. However, at this point the Universe knows what you're trying to achieve and will assist even if you decide to not utilize the fabric in any way.

Put everything inside, together with some "wishes" that you've written on red felt. Give them good wishes. are sure to make come true! (All according to the divine timing)

Divine timing is when the Universe provides us with our desires but at its own pace. Most of the time, it is when it's not happening when it like we are in need of it. Be patient, abundance is coming! Promise. The good thing is the more attentive we are, the more evidence we see! :)

Chapter 17: Vision Board Instructions For The Vision Board

Making a vision board is one of my most recommended activities to take part in. I am amazed at each year, I create them , and how they come to fruition. In this Vision Board I put everything connected to Feng Shui Map. Visualize that you are putting the Feng Shui Map over my Vision Board. Love is found in the Love region and also in the similar colors, Wealth is also the same, and so on.

This board will be focusing on those aspects of Prosperity as well as Abundance. Make the entire board about wealth and Blessings. You can also make use of Google Picassa to create a collage for your screensaver that will keep track of your goals. Have fun and write down what your top goals are in the context of what and let the Universe will provide in surprising ways. Do not limit yourself with negative self-talk "I will never have that car or vacation." You never have a clue when a new opportunity will arise and help you realize your goals.

The alternative is to buy an artist canvas at the dollar store, along with several images. You can either get them from magazines or photographs you've taken, or even from the web and print them. Adhere or stick each photo onto the canvas to create an art collage. Have fun! Imagine big and then put an incredibly deserved vacation on the table. The time off is a source of prosperity too! Let your creative juices flow as abundance flowing toward you!

Create a Word document that includes your most favorite phrases or daily affirmations. I love these kinds of affirmations.

Money flows easily to me and in many surprising ways.

I am open and ready to receive abundance on every level and in a variety of ways.

Money is my favorite thing! And Money loves me!

Ich am a money Magnet!

I am extremely happy and thankful to have received "fill with the missing" and much more than I anticipated.

I have the ability at the moment to create the wealth I've always wanted. And I deserve it.

I have a clientele who value me and willing be willing to pay for my services.

Chapter 18: The 1000 Thank-You Challenge

Begin a gratitude journal and keep track of minimum 10 items per day. If I really want to get something going I record 100 days in a row. This is equivalent to 1000 thank-you's over one week for my Universe which always responds with a lovely surprise.

To get into the state of being energetic enough to experience more abundance and gratitude, it is essential. Try it I am sure you will see a significant shift in the way you feel, and you will discover that gifts appear in the blink of an eye.

I am always grateful to the Universe and Creator to be healthy, my friends, opportunities to wake up, my comfy bed I sleep in and my car that takes me around with fashion, a pleasant conversation, a gorgeous day I'm sure you can get the picture.

Chapter 19: Here Are 35 Steps To Reduce Your Monthly Expenses From Today!

These are useful strategies to accumulate or save money. They are not intended to make you feel bad, they're designed to make you feel better and feel in control of your financial situation.

1 Contact every service provider you have and request better rates at minimal cost. You will get more than the amount you already pay. It may sound crazy but they'll lower rates by 7 of 10. Contact the lender (the contact number can be found listed on the back of your card) and ask for lower interest rates. A single percent could save you thousands or hundreds over time. If they don't agree immediately, ask to speak to the manager or threaten to move your company elsewhere. Prepare yourself to take this action by calling around and comparing who has lower rates and inquire if they are willing to transfer the balance, etc. Make a call to your mobile

phone company. I was able to get $10 off each month due to an unintentional call for 5 minutes and also got an additional feature. It saves me $120 a year. Nice! If after the first time your service provider does not say no then try it again. It really does matter who you're speaking to and how content they are on that particular day.

2. Be organized while shopping and follow the loop. Instead of taking a trip from A to B and then back to A and then across to C, back to A, and finally return to F. (for Been frustrated that you've been driving all across town fighting the traffic and using up gas.) Make your plans for your trips with the car and make use of non-peak travel hours whenever you can, which means less traffic and less waiting. Instead of traveling to the same location twice a week, reasons that aren't related, is it possible to just go once to save on fuel. Find out where you're going, and make sure you visit all locations in the same area in the same day at times that aren't busy

and you'll be driving with pleasure again! It also grants you valuable time back.

3. Sell any non-useable "good to give away to someone else" things to raise money.

4. Become an affiliate of the products or services that you love and recommend them to your family and friends. It is only possible when you believe in this product/service. It could result in some extra money or even services for you! Bonus! Many websites that are part in Affiliate programs include a link to the bottom of the page and can join for free. You can then share it on Facebook, Twitter it, and pin it for profit!

5. Be clear on the amount you have to pay. This is the initial step to tackle any financial concern. If you require an expert financial advisor, do it immediately, and don't wait until the situation is so dire that you are receiving calls from anywhere and causing additional anxiety. Each consolidation office offers free

consultations for new clients and will offer advice at

at the very least, get a professional's review of your next step will be. Write it down.

6. Be aware of your numbers! What is the amount of interest you are paying and how much? If you are owed money on credit, pay off the interest that is highest first until the debt is gone. Next, you can start with the next interest and so on.

7 - Take charge of your vision of financial wellbeing. Visit your bank and discuss your account. Consider other banks that offer smaller transaction costs and higher rates of interest for savings. Consolidate as quickly as you can. This will reduce interest payments which drain your bank account!

8 Make sure you pay yourself first! Yes, I understand you...how do I pay for this when there's not enough. Let me share my thoughts. There will be no money if you

don't take this simple process. Read the Wealthy Barber by David Chilton.

9 - Set financial goals. I'll increase my earnings by 25 percent. So, make it happen. This doesn't mean that you have to work longer hours. Be creative.

10 Place your credit card in ice, literally, so that you can end your spending! I once frozen my credit card inside an insulated Tupperware container in order to end from making poor choices. Put it away for a brief period and observe the change.

11. Write down each penny you pay. Make note of it! Find out where you can save money.

12 Bring your own cup of coffee to work. Lattes and coffees increase each month. If you drink one cup of coffee every day at 2.50 cups, that's $650 dollars per year! It's like the equivalent of a holiday! It also allows you to spend more time.

13 Pack your own lunch. Not just healthier, but much more attractive to carry around in your pocket!

14 Make a commitment to yourself...if you require an additional training course to enhance your abilities in order to get that promotion, then go for the opportunity! The increase will pay for the course in the future. If you're an entrepreneur, find the help of a professional coach, one that is successful one who will give you the best strategies to attract clients quickly! You should choose a coach who you have done your research and has proven reliable results. Take a marketing course or whatever you can to make money come in. If you're thinking I cannot afford it, Mila...can you afford to carry on in the same way? In your business, if you're not expanding your dying. Grow! Make the decision to be prosperous and soon you'll become successful. Anyone can acquire business knowledge but you require the right coach or teacher for you.

15 If you own your own home, put an energy saving blanket over the water heater. The blankets for water heaters cost about 35 dollars and can cost you around 90 dollars in a single year. About 3 KW of energy each day. It is able to pay for itself in only 4 months , and is very simple to set up.

16 Set up an rain barrel to capture rain water. In summer, you are able to plant your garden using rain water, that is healthier for plants and also saves money on your water bill. It also helps the environment. Win, win, win.

17 - Grow your own vegetables. Delicious, fresh , and inexpensive! There are vegetables to be grown virtually all over the world, so take your time and you can learn. It's fun and rewarding and you are aware of exactly where your food comes from.

18 ~ Fix your leaky faucets. The smallest drip adds to a lot.

19 Turn the temperature down by a couple of degrees at the very least before you go to sleep. This small change could add hundreds of dollars in savings throughout the year. Install a thermostat that can be programmed to control the temperature without having to think about it. When you're working, set it to increase the temperature you are on your way home, and cool off in the evening when you go to sleep. A couple of degrees cooler in the evening will allow you to sleep better!

20 Make use of baking soda as well as vinegar to make the earth-friendly cleaning agents.

21 ~ Use your local library! The entire library of books and knowledge you'll need at no cost, as well as DVD's.

22 Buy an reusable water bottle and make use of it! It also helps the environment and you will save at least $2.00/day.

23 Make your own meals.

24 Purchase refurbished electronic devices that have been fixed and usually at cheaper prices than those at retail stores. Additionally, you should only purchase items being sold!

25 Create a shopping list of your grocery purchases and adhere to it! It's incredible how much items cost if you're uncertain about what you should buy and you are in the store in a hurry and don't know what you're looking for in an item.

26. Don't cut corners on regular maintenance for your vehicle. This will save you a lot of money in the near future.

27. Switch off the lights and unplug your appliances, chargers printers, and other household appliances when you aren't making use of them. They can drain the energy of our pockets if we're not vigilant.

28 Plan for expenses such as birthday gifts and night out. Put aside a small amount each month , so that when the happy occasions show up, you'll have enough to

enjoy yourself and your loved ones. You know you deserve!

29 Eat Vegetarian at least one every week. I eat a variety of vegetables about 70 percent of all the time. It's a healthy choice not one for money. I believe that Health = Wealth

30 Purchase quality clothes that last and feature timeless fashion.

31 Treat yourself to an indulgence Don't be cheap, just smart!

32 Purchase drought-resistant plants to reduce outdoor water use

33 Draft proof your home! Find some caulking or silicone for the doors and windows, and weather stripping for your exterior doors are two locations to start.

34 In the summer make sure to shade your windows so that the house remains cool.

35 - Keep your car's trunk free of clutter. If it's stuffed with stuff, the extra weight will cost more fuel.

So I've figured out the amount you could save If you packed yourself a lunch and bought coffee, used an reusable water bottle, and only paid 10 per month on your mobile bill . The final total is... $290. WOW! Like this!

I calculated this based on a five-day work week that lasts for 260 consecutive days of the year.

Lunch $5 + 130 equals 1300 (that is an estimate of lunch at a lower cost too)

Drinking water - 2 dollars x 2260 equals the sum of 520 (on water)

Coffee -- $2.50 + 260 = 650

The Mobile Bill Discount is $10 12 x 10 equals 120

Your savings are 1300 + 120 = $2590

Doesn't that make sense?

These guidelines aren't designed to make you live a life without but rather to help you live your life. Make sure you are smart about your money and it will increase.

Being proactive and smart about spending doesn't just increase your wealth but also allows you to feel more confident in yourself and boost your self-esteem. If you work hard to earn your money, so keep it! If you make your payments, you will feel good about repaying it in complete. If you shop, be in the excitement of spending, and know that you'll earn additional money. It's a continuous flow of Cashola If you allow it to be!

Chapter 20: Mind Set And The Law Of Attraction!

Setting the right mindset is vital for our achievement. If we live thinking that there's no way to be enough this is precisely what we'll get. You must think a lot of thoughts, stay optimistic, know exactly what you want to achieve without doubt, and be confident that it was already there precisely at the right time.

Connect with positivity-filled people. Only let positive things to enter your life. The more I turn off the TV and concentrate upon positive thoughts, affirmations ideas of books, actions and concentrate on what I truly want, it all comes together in the most beautiful and amazing way. It falls right onto your doorstep! The people you associate with can definitely impact your attitude and the ability of you to take a step forward in the right direction.

A quick note on letting go of the current "friends" who hinder your progress. When you begin to grow and change your financial obstacles to the mindset of being able to enjoy abundantly on all levels, like excellent health, lots of time, and more money you'll encounter resistance from the people who are around you. They are stuck with their own financial issues or they are simply unable to comprehend the concept that money can effortlessly flow into your life. I've found that I needed remove these individuals in my life whom I have dubbed "energy suckers". These are the people I'm talking about, the "friends who call only when they're having problems or when they want you to take action for them , or when they require to get money. By transforming your financial vibration, you are making your life more balanced and it is essential not to allow them pull you down or cause doubt in your head. The biggest problem with it is when you become worried about what you need instead of focusing on your own. I am convinced that you have the ability to do or do anything you like however it requires determination, perseverance and persistence as well as a strategy filled with actions to take.

The first step to transforming your abundance is knowing precisely what you would like to achieve. If you do not have an end desired outcome in mind, how will you determine the steps you need to take in order to reach that goal? I'm able to give you an example. I'm in need of more money, whereas I'll increase my income by 25% in the coming year has two completely different perceptions. The first I'm looking for more money does not have a final result that is monetary in nature and there's no specific approach to achieving the target. The statement that I'm going to increase my earnings by 25 percent by the end this year, you could be sure to take the necessary action by determining the number of new clients you'll require to reach that goal, or innovative workshop that you are developing or perhaps a part-time job or a different method to earn passive income. there's a dollar amount and you must to set a deadline or else you'll do things later. This later date will never come.

Do not use the word "need" If you're in the category of "need" money, you are always in need of it. Replace this pattern of thinking by saying I have plenty of money, since you already have it, and then include the statement that"I am willing to accept" abundance in any form, like money, checks, and other easy to put into practice money making strategies.

Here are some questions you can consider asking yourself to determine precisely what you're looking for.

How much money do I want? Start with per calendar year and before breaking it down into months and then to daily.

What should I do with that extra cash?

What kind of vacation would I like to take?

What do I think I can do with my time off?

What charity would I like to donate to?

What kind of house should I get when I buy a house?

How can I behave differently?

What kind of vehicle do I want?

What kind of pet should I be able to bring with me?

Where would you like to live If you could move, would you?

What's the average wage I earn?

What type of food do I consume?

Where should I go to eat dinner?

What sort of clothes do you prefer to wear?

Imagine your life the way you'd like it.

Then ask yourself what is you are preventing you...what are your beliefs that limit you about money? Are you averse to it? The only way to say that money is available for people is by a bank. But neither of these are the case. Sure, there are some bad wealthy people However, there are amazing people who love helping others in need. The truth is that money is not evil. it's neither good or bad , it is just a way to purchase what we desire. It's also important to note that it doesn't have to be difficult to obtain also, so let go of the notion that it is difficult to get. It's easy and enjoyable to make great cash! In addition, you should be able to earn the amount of money you want. Be aware that you deserve it! Repetition this mantra to yourself, it will help shift your mind.

My guess is that there is nothing stopping you! You have the ability and resources to accomplish this. Really. Plan it out, follow the necessary actions and follow through!

Keep in mind that you can't fail. It is possible to quit. But that's not what you should do, is it?

It is a matter of choice. You can choose to be successful.

The most effective way to aid others is by helping yourself. Imagine where you could contribute and help those causes you truly love and would like to help, however you may not be able to do so right now. How would it feel being comfortable with your relationship to money?

Therefore, focus on you! Concentrate your attention on something which makes you feel happy and joyful. Concentrate on the positive things that you are experiencing in your life already. Concentrate on the things you love doing, and cash will be a natural result. It has worked for me. I switched from being a home stager/designer to becoming a Tarot Reader because I found that I was working for too long hours and running around town, which eventually resulted in me becoming exhausted. In that time, I picked up a Tarot deck and enjoyed it. I was enthralled about learning about it. When you told me that I was going to be an Tarot Reader 5 years ago I'd told you it was a joke. When I started reading the Tarot I didn't know that it would become an enterprise for me. None! I simply followed my heart and took baby steps to expand my business, and it has been a long and rewarding journey that has included numerous blessings, trials and difficulties. But what do you know? I've learned a lot from my failings, perhaps more than my victories. I love winning, but don't forget the lessons.

These are all fantastic exercise in visioning and I would like you to dream Big but be realistic here. Take pictures of your answers and place your answers on the Vision Board and look at each throughout the day. It's on the way...you are granted this Dream because it's feasible! I can assure you that the Universe provided you with a means to make this dream occur, pay attention to your dreams, ideas and the endless conversations. If you are attentive to what you are hearing, the answer is in front of you and only you will know the answer! These thoughts or concepts that pop up are divinely granted and won't be a burden. However, you must be attentive and then take action on the ideas or thoughts. Even the smallest of steps can lead you to the next step and the next step, etc. Do what you love and it will all come together. Most importantly, take action with your ideas and your intuitions.

All you have to do is take first steps. There is no need to be aware of everything about the journey Just begin. Let me say this: you deserve every ounce of abundance in the World and you are a loved by the Universe. The Universe will give you everything you desire. It's not just the money but the flexibility and time or being capable of letting your mind drift away from the expenses or even take a vacation. Your desires will become your reality if you have the right goals.

Chapter 21: Goal Setting Tips

The first step is to think about how your ideal life could appear to be like. Simply think about the ultimate outcome. Answer the above questions in the most vivid way you can.

Utilize this Tool You may have heard of this before , but it's the best advice

S Then, with a specificity you get the final result.

M - Measurable, which means you can see the distinction.

A Attainable and Action be confident that you will achieve it, be aware of the actions.

R Relevant, how does it aid your situation?

T Tracking and Timing What is your time frame as well as who's your accountable partner?

Make sure you put your goals down in writing, and use the most positive language you could. Instead of for instance, declaring that I would like $100,000 to fall into my lap. Tell me that I am open and ready to hear about my $100,000 (or higher) idea or an inspiration, and when you get the big idea or inspiration, ACT ON IT! I will put "my 100,000 idea" into action in the next (fill in the date) is immediately. Start aligning yourself with Abundance, work hard and be creative. Get outdoors, and be in the joy of living and abundance. Inspire yourself with positive words and only watch positive content on TV, and be around positive people. You must be within the Abundance zone in order to receive it.

Reduce it to small objectives. One is that you can recognize the difference but that aren't overpowering.

Create your Action Steps and add it to the Calendar. Make time and plan each hour to accomplish these objectives. You must organize and plan your success. It isn't enough to note it down and hope it to come to you by magic. It requires some effort.

A large part of getting what you desire in the abundance aspect of your life boils down to goal-setting. It is essential to set an amount of money each month, and even regularly when you are working independently. Follow the actions of contacting your customers and applying for jobs, seeking out new ways to earn money, learning about marketing, and start an inexpensive business or be afraid to test new things. Even if you don't succeed or your marketing strategy does not go as planned, it's at least an important lesson. It didn't go as planned. Failure will lead to achievement. Be sure to keep your passion determination, determination, drive, perseverance, or focus. Whatever you've accomplished in your life has brought you to this moment, and each experience is important and will be of use in the near future. You will then experience one of those moments where you think to yourself, you're the reason that it took place!

Chapter 22: The Power Of Crystal Gemstones

What is the reason why Gemstones work...I consider that everything has energy. If you didn't, you wouldn't have this book. When our energy is sucked to the energy of a lack or a slow pace, it's just a matter of giving it a bit of a kick. Imagine your aura around you , but it's not completely. There are tiny holes within your field of energy. What Gemstones can do is to fill in the gaps. Each Crystal has their own DNA, just like us and has this energy. Like us, we carry our own personal energy. You've experienced this before. If you spot someone extremely angry, you can see it in the room. Similar to when the people around you are enjoying a great time, and you feel the same good-feeling energy. The Gemstones simply add that joyous element and, as an DNA Band-Aid so to speak and you're back to being complete. These tiny Crystal Gemstones are really powerful and actually perform. They are quite scientific, actually. Here are a few of my suggestions for the Abundance space within your residence. You can take them on your person, set these in the Prosperity Jar or put an emerald in your wallet , to ensure you always have money and be content when you spend. You can buy any number or small as you want. I would suggest getting one of of the five I have listed here, and placing them in your wealth area and the citrine to hold in your wallet. Once you have them, take them out, and take a look do you feel that it is begging to return to you? Each gem is unique in its own way and, just as when you meet someone, they could either touch you in a negative way or create the instant bond. Try to find the connection to your precious stones.

You can find these treasures in any nearby Metaphysical Shop or order them on the internet.

Five of my favorite tools for manifesting abundance.

Citrine color yellow and Clear occasionally brown

It is a beautiful Gem Citrine is beautiful! It is a joy-seeker and money-maker, and it raises our vibration towards happier and peaceful times. Because this Gem protects the earth and our Aura it absorbs negative energy and simply takes it away. Thanks, Citrine.

Since it is said that in Feng Shui the Element for Wealth is Wood, it's crucial to do everything we can to help the environment. This stone helps us to ground ourselves and alerts us when something is not right. It increases our intuition and helps us find the way to success.

Additionally This Gem is a cleanser and purifier of our Chakras. Restoring Balance.

Citrine lets us be ourselves without becoming too sensitive. Instead of being upset when someone else suggests something, Citrine lets us take action when we are confronted with criticism.

This crystal boosts self-esteem, self-confidenceand an increase in creativity, assists you in maintaining positive attitudes and assists in releasing our fears and limits that we put on ourselves without a reason.

Citrine speaks with our intuition and urges it to whisper into our ears, giving us the faith to listen. That's huge. This is where the million dollar ideas originate. This stone is good for all things.

Citrine does not require to be cleaned, it does it by itself. Citrine is a shade that fades when exposed to sunlight, so be cautious about when you place it!

Carnelian Color: Red, Orange, Pink and Brown

Carnelian is known as the "Great motivator" Stone! If you're in need of some motivation, energy, stand up and head towards this gem.

This Gemstone eliminates fear and lets you go away from self-limiting convictions.

This strong Crystal helps you to clear your mind and inspires you to conquer and truly take on yourself!

Carnelian stimulates your base or root Chakra and improves the fertility of your body and also brings your sexual desire back to action. Be aware! (Just kidding, I'm slightly serious.) Actually, this stone assists you in your creativity and boosts your energy. This is a great way to "birth" fresh ideas that are our own creations. If you're in business for yourself, this is a good way to guard yourself against and perhaps discontent you're earning all the money! When people notice your progress. Don't allow anyone to steal your light. Shine bright and leave those negative nellies to dust!

Green Aventurine: Can be red, blue, green brown and peach.

We're employing Green to represent the color of nature and money.

Green Aventurine continues the theme of Joy in the way we create our cashola! The stone is said to be very fortunate when it comes to Feng Shui! Since it's green, like it is the colour of wealth, and the color of fresh beginnings, this is a highly beneficial stone for anyone.

This gemstone helps us develop compassion for others and ourselves when we are growing and establishing our relationship with money. It helps us take clear action steps to follow and help us become the person we're meant to be. The color green Aventurine is a potent heart chakra healer. It assists in balancing our lives and calms doubts about ourselves.

Aventurine offers us the chance to examine what's effective and what's not working. It provides us with options, alternatives or a new concept to help our dreams and talents emerge. Here is where I'd like to point out that whether you're in the industry, it is vital to our achievement. It is essential to be able to be resilient and take on the sand. Every marketing strategy is not successful so we need to understand why it failed, then modify and attempt again! This can be the measure of success! The more you experiment and the more opportunities arise and the more you learn the things that work. On the other hand, you can tell what doesn't work, mean you have to go through that process again. This is a win for itself!

This stone can also be extremely effective in protecting electromagnetic energy like your cell phone or laptop.

Furthermore, this unique Gem allows us to live from the place that is our heart. It is our true goal of what we were created to do was to serve our careers. It's all an absolute Gem

The Red Tiger's Eye: Brown, Red Blue, Pink with streaks in Yellow or Gold

To achieve this, I'd make use of the brown or red colored gem.

Red Tigers Eye is great for connecting with the Source and Divine Energy. If you're seeking answers to your financial issues, put the Gem in your third eye, and then meditate on the issue. Be still and calm then place your Gem in the middle until you receive an answer from the heavens. It's always a success! Take a moment to ask, listen, and then find the solution and put it into practice.

Like the name implies, this Crystal is about vision, visioning , and keeping our vision of wealth. (Life in general too!) This is an effective balancer, too. This gem helps us make swift decisions and assists us in achieving the goals we've recorded.

Tiger`s Eye unsticks stuck thinking or lack of imagination. The ability to open up your mind and increase conversations with Spirit. It also helps you to see your incredible extraordinary and distinctive abilities. This boosts your sense of confidence in yourself and boosts self-esteem. The eye of Tiger aids us to recognize our strengths and the best ways to contribute to our community.

This Gemstone connects us with that Earth Energy needed to receive Prosperity. Ideal for letting go of old habits that have held us back from the beginning. Additionally, it gives those who are lost or confused an uncluttered mind that can discern what is a Wish or what is your real purpose in life. It's pretty powerful stuff!

Amethyst Color: From Purple Lavender

Amethyst has numerous wonderful properties. It is one of the Gemstones to heal the body. This Gemstone I have included here specifically to solve our money problems. If it's about boosting levels of income, getting rid of debt or simply an increase in our wealth.

This Gemstone protects us from the negative energies and eliminates our "blocks" which allows us to be free to take a step forward. Amethyst helps to calm our brains that are over-active and allows us to come up with new thoughts and then follow through with the ideas. It gives us the knowledge we've been looking for.

Our strategy! Five of these Gems together offer us the strength we need to overcome our fears , and overcome our fears and realize our dreams. This helps us in getting what we want.

Amethyst can also help us develop our Psychic abilities , allowing us to truly listen to the inner voice that knows exactly what we should do. (Our Instinctual Wisdom or Higher Self) This then lets us enjoy the moment and envision the future we want to see, increase the motivation to do so and lessens fears so that we can actually do what we say. What a gem!

Chapter 23: Cleaning Your Gemstones

Before we can place your Gems inside the Wealth Corner, we need to clean them and then make them active. It's a breeze. We simply need to take the gems you have in your hands and place them in cold water, for at minimum 30 minutes. When you place them in the water, set your intention to use these Gemstones. You can say with your mouth, "These Gems will aid me in keeping Wealth within my reach. Thank you for assisting me in my journey and I am sure that Wealth is already here."

Alternately, if it's just around the time of the time of a Full or New Moon we can place the gemstones in a bowl of water and place them on a window over night. The Moon is huge and extremely powerful. It gives vitality to Gems as well as providing an extra sense of intuition to us as well as the Gems.

A New Moon is a great time to establish goals. It adds that extra oomph to any and any dream.

Another option can be to bring the Gems to the river or the beach along with you. Simply dip them in for a brief period of time, then create the intention of your choice.

You can't be doing this wrong. So long as you're doing your best, the Universe is aware and will support you.

Write your dreams and goals out and keep them in a safe place to be able to read and repeat them regularly. Writing your own note in the direction of the Universe is incredibly effective. I promise.

When you feel you desire to cleanse, repeat the Gemstone cleaning process over and over at least once.

Place your gems in either Your Prosperity Jar as well as in the Wealth Area. If you are able to take them with you for a short period of time, make sure to do this. I have a variety of Gems in my pockets, purses, and around my home.

Make sure you place one or two gems that you're most attracted to on your computer screen. I personally love my Green Aventurine on my desk.

Be sure to enjoy the information you've learned. The more you are able to enjoy abundance, when you are when you are in a state of happiness you're.

Chapter 24: Reasons Why We Require Feng Shui

After you have a better knowledge of Feng Shui as described in the introduction, I'd like to walk you through step-by-step through the reasons why you require Feng Shui in order to see transformations to your lifestyle. It is possible to think that something is not right, but how do you determine what the issue is?

Do you ever feel that all the world is in opposition to your plans? If so, Feng Shui could be the best solution.

There are many who believe that what's meant to be will eventually be. Others believe that we don't have any control over our destiny. Others believe that God has a plan created for each one of us.

We can't be able to tell which of these principles are correct however, Feng Shui can aid us in increasing the positive energy in our lives. It might not be the ideal solution for all issues, but there's nothing wrong with exploring a bit of Feng Shui. It is possible that we have a specific destiny to achieve, but with Feng Shui, it is possible to enhance the direction we'll be following on our life.

Feng Shui can help us develop an equilibrium in our lives. Achieving balance will help us improve our own health and well-being. It also assists us attain positive and desired results.

Fundamental FENG SHUI CONCEPTS OF FENG SHUI and THE PRINCIPLES

Feng Shui as a complex art is made up of a variety of theories and ideas.

THE PRINCIPLES

*Chi Chi

It is the energy that lives or the breath of the earth. It is absorbed by all things that exists. Positive Chi can give a person or object the positivity and wellbeing. However negative chi creates malignancies and illness within the body of a person.

Feng Shui can be interpreted as the correct channels of Chi. People and objects must be placed in an enlightening location to attract good luck. Chi is required to be balanced and allow to flow smoothly throughout the space to bring happiness and wellbeing.

*Ba Gua Area

Ba Gua is comprised of eight sides, which represent the eight directions to guide Feng Shui. Eight Ba Gua areas are North, Northeast, East, SouthEast, South, Southwest, West and Northwest. A home has the eight Ba Gua areas that can be adjusted to suit the desires of the owner. The individual Ba Gua area can be remedied by using ornaments and colors in order to attain favorable Feng Shui.

*Three types of Ba Gua

There are three kinds of Ba Gua, the flat concave, convex and flat. They are utilized to serve different reasons. Be cautious when making use of these three kinds of Ba Gua.

1. Flat Ba Gua can be used as an ongoing Feng Shui tool. It is to be placed over the entrance, or if it is not in the door within the door. Make sure that it's not inside. It serves as an instrument to balance the flow of chi . It safeguards the house and people living there from negative and harmful vibrations.

2. A convex Ba Gua is used as an instrument to temporarily diffuse and disperse negative chi, also known as shar chi that can result from incorrect placement of homes or entrances. A prime example is when the door is facing the sharp edge of a different structure, road or even a tree.

3. Concave Ba Gua can also be an effective tool that can be used to block the negative energies and stop it from entering your home.

*Elements

Feng Shui uses the 5 elements to guide the user and to fix a poor Feng Shui environment. Five Feng Shui elements include Earth Metal, Water, Fire and Wood. Five elements interact each other , causing destruction or increase productivity.

Certain elements are compatible with one element, while other elements are in conflict with and destroy one another. To ensure harmony and balance between elements, the objects of one element should be placed in the correct Ba Gua area. People born in an element should be in a relationship together with someone from an element which feeds his particular element.

*Colors

Utilizing colors is another method to improve Feng Shui the house or within the case of an individual. Each of the five Feng Shui elements are represented with the appropriate colors.

1. Earth light brown earth tones light yellow

2. Blue, black

3. Fire - red, orange dark pink, yellow,

4. Metal Gray, White

5. Wood brown or green

The birth of a person is the year that has a similar element. To ensure you get the most fulfilling life and destiny you should wear the right colors to complement your particular element. If you were born during the Year for the Water Dog, you must wear jewelry and clothes with black or blue colors.

*Numbers

The importance of numbers is also for Feng Shui. There are certain numbers that can bring luck to a specific Ba Gua area. Numerology has various interpretations within Feng Shui. The number 1 signifies beginnings. The number 8 signifies infinite or inexhaustible prosperity. The number 9 signifies abundance or abundance.

*Lunar Year

It is believed that the Chinese lunar calendar plays part when it comes to the art of Feng Shui. People born in a particular year should be cautious when selecting the right partner.

To have a happy relationship, you should pick a person who is born during a similar year. The people's Chinese zodiacs can also influence their behavior and attitudes as well as how they interact with others. People who belong to a specific Chinese zodiac should also be aware of the best Ba Gua direction to sleep or live.

In this way they can be sure to enjoy a restful sleep, healthier as well as a successful career, and general happiness. These are only a few of the principles and concepts which are employed when practicing Feng Shui. Feng Shui experts can help you get the right result using their vast expertise, knowledge and understanding of this art form.

The concept of collaborating to create positive changes

Warm Welcome Warm Welcome - In Feng Shui, the main entry point to the house is a crucial part which requires focus. This is the place where the chi flows in and out all throughout the home. The most fundamental idea is to have the entrance properly placed in the right direction. It will also help create an appearance that is inviting and warm.

To be successful in your career, you should utilize the blue color on the North Ba Gua area.

*Chinese Coins: Take an 18 or 9 inch (or any other multiple of nine) the red ribbon. Use it to connect three Chinese coins together. This can help draw the money to your home. Hang it on the knob or handle on the rear of your door.

It is recommended to apply white color on your western Ba Gua area of your house to boost your creative abilities.

Beware of sharp corners in your home as they can disrupt the flow of the chi. Try softening them by placing some plants in the corners.

To improve the health and well-being of families The East Ba Gua area of the home must be decorated or painted with plants or green ornaments.

It is also possible to add blue to ensure it is well-nourished. The water element helps nourish it's wood elements.

* Get rid of clutter in your home. Maintain your home as neat and neat as you can. It gives a peaceful and positive atmosphere.

Avoid placing a mirror in the bed in front of you.

Fix anything that is damaged promptly. If something is broken, leaky or filthy can cause negative energy in your home.

For happiness and a happy social life, choose a bright yellow color on the Southern portion of your house.

*Place an object or plant over the window to separate the interior of your home from the outside. This is the best method to do particularly when the window faces the street or a vacant lot.

Be sure to keep the ceiling fans and beams off from your favourite spot like the couch or bed. They act as poisonous the arrows or a burden on your energy. Take out the fan or cover beams to block the negative impact.

Place your desk in a spot where allows you to see the front of the room or home. If you aren't able to then, consider putting up an angled mirror so that you are capable of seeing the blind areas.

*Do not place your bed in an open window.

Take away items that make you think of your failure, and replace them with decorations that bring back your achievements and your passions.

Avoid sitting in a chair with an air duct over it. If you can't move your chair, figure out ways you can cover up the air duct. Or redirect it away from shoulders by using an apron.

Be at one with nature. Include plants, flowers and pets to your house because they bring positive energy.

Use the bedroom to rest and the office for work. This is common sense and doesn't be in contradiction to the idea of yin and Yang. Everyone wants to not feel exhausted while at work or tired at night.

*Open a door inside your office to let air circulate and enter. This will allow you to feel more energized.

*Collect decorations from similar elements in a grouping to give a greater appearance. For instance, you can put fish bowls and fountains, or incense and candles next to each one.

Always place your chairs in a place with the doors facing you. This will allow you to have an unobstructed view of your entrance in the event that there is an intrusion.

- Put up positive decorations inside your home like family photos, photos of your friends' group achievements certificates as well as other reminders of your happy times and personal achievements. Avoid self-portraits to avoid feeling lonely.

*Place wind chimes on pathways or corridors to enhance the flow of Chi.

Set your mirrors on gorgeous windows or beautiful views. This can attract and encourage positive energy.

Three potted plants are ideal for putting red flowers on the pathway towards your front door.

Take away any unsafe furniture from your home. Select furniture with soft , rounded edges.

Decorate your home with fresh flowers, candles and live plants. This will increase the warmth, vitality and comfort of your home.

- Store food items in your cupboards in order to create an abundance feeling.

Do not place aquarium fish inside the bedroom, bathroom, or the kitchen. In doing this, you could result in damage to the property.

The sofas should be arranged in a circular fashion so you have a chance to talk.

Be sure to place the television in the middle of your living room.

Place a pond in your house , and add eight carps of red or gold as well as one carp that is black. The black carp will absorb negative energy instead of letting them be absorbed by the person who lives in the home.

Chapter 25: Using Feng Shui To Completely Eliminate Obstaclesin Your Life

Feng Shui help you have the ability to be mindful of objects in your surroundings that create obstructions in your daily life. They aren't just tangible objects such as tables, couches or computer and also those psychological "clutter" that prevents you from being mindful and hinders you from realizing your highest potential in your life.

What does a "cutter" really mean?

It's likely that you don't know that the majority of this mess is the result of an emotional, although no longer relevant attachment. When you start to get rid of the clutter from your home and your home, you will also let go of old attachments to things which no longer provide you with satisfaction.

You could, for instance, keep an old tennis shoe that you used to wear on a particular date, but as the relationship didn't work out and the shoes aren't working, you're keeping something that's not an integral part of your life. These habits can keep you from enjoying a fulfilling new one, since psychologically, you're hanging an attachment to the past.

If you start to take off years of clutter in your attic, you might be surprised by the amount of stuff from your past has held you back from your dreams. Because the attic symbolizes larger goals or goals so it's not surprising it can feel as if you've failed to achieve all that you could have in the past.

This is what the art of Feng Shui does. It will make you think about making choices based on your real intention.

Fear and Hoarding

Don't undervalue the power of anxiety. When you go through the piles of old clothing, records albums books, knickknacks, and other items you might wonder what you've done with all these things for many years. Did you think of using them in the future? Most likely not. In fact, you may not have considered letting go of your past because of your uncertain outlook on the future.

Between job shifts, multiple changes, or the various phases that couples go through, the prospect being unable to have the resources money to be able to survive is a major issue for a lot of people. People in a state of continuous change tend to find solace in their emotional hoarding. They gather things to calm the soul, which is longing for love and hoping to find the satisfaction that money cannot purchase.

Oft, they don't know that they're doing it until they've accumulated lots of things within their home that barely breathe! If you want to have the best Feng Shui in your home it is essential to be sure to take a hard review of yourself and your requirements and eliminate the things that are no longer serving you.

Hoarding of emotions isn't limited to objects. The similar principles that govern Feng Shui clearing apply to the "clutter" people store in their bodies. It's not a surprise that people who are overweight are afflicted by the same psychological issues as other kinds of hoarders, and are afflicted by the same fear about not being able to get enough.

What's interesting is those who are hoarders and clutter-aholics begin to learn about excellent Feng Shui and relinquish their accumulations of clutter, a lot are also beginning to shed weight.

A Constant Process

Integrating Feng Shui into your lifestyle and mental outlook is a continuous process. It could take years before you are aware that you're content confident, secure and safe. Continuously evaluate where you're at and what you require and you'll soon be facing the clutter dragon.

It will be clear that it's the right time for an enormous purge, both psychologically and physically. And what a wonderful feeling it is to let go of your worries or the failures from the past!

If you are taking a more in-depth study of the emotional connections you've made to the past, be sure to look at the other sources of clutter within your home. Consider clutter in the garage and basement, the hallway closets, and even inside your car. If you look more closely at the circumstances What can you learn about your habits of clutter?

Many things -- for example the mess in your basement, for instance, symbolizes unrest within your family life as the basement is a symbol of family and stability. Feng Shui is symbolic of solid foundations and family.

The clutter in your garage could indicate a psychological issue leaving the house each day, or when you return home. If you're unable to get out of your garage due to piles of clutter, be thinking about what you're not able to return to in your daily life.

However, if you're a true homebody and you've stuffed yourself in your garage with the clutter, it might be the time to start your own home-based company so that you can stay at home more often however in a more healthy way.

The best way to deal with clutter is being capable of taking these types of hard look at your personal desires, and needs to discover the reasons behind what you're keeping.

Abundance and prosperity

The most fundamental aspect of studying Feng Shui, and metaphysics generally is the concept of constant abundance. Through the concept of prosperity consciousness, as it's also known the more you give, the more you're open to receiving.

There is nothing that says "I may require it in the future," because as soon when you donate something it creates a place for anything that is new and urgently needed. If you allow yourself to the anxiety of not having enough, you'll lead a life where there is never enough to feel satisfied.

Instead, change your perspective to acknowledge the present moment with regard to your current situation. Your life will be successful since you'll draw positive abundance.

It's a very simple idea however, it's difficult for many to master without constant training. It could take a few years to see your life, and yourself from this point of view every day.

One of the most fundamental principles of metaphysics (often considered to be the work of karma) can be that the energy you give towards the Universe is what you receive in return.

Therefore, if you declare to the Universe that you're going to be unhealthy and in poor shape this is the kind of life you'll build for yourself based on your personal limitations in mind. The real beauty of life lies in the beliefs you hold regarding what you believe you are capable of achieving.

Becoming a victim of a Clutter-aholics

The piles are upon the ground, hidden (or packed) beneath furniture or rest at a precarious height in a corner. You're looking to tidy your home But there's an issue This stuff is yours. It's someone who has a pile of their own.

What should you do? Begin by contacting your client in a polite way and offering assistance to get rid of the items. People are extremely insecure about their possessions and belongings, so don't simply begin putting things away or throw them in the garbage. Be respectful of your family member's desire for privacy and security.

You can get to where the issue lies issue by asking yourself a few inquiries: "Does this still serve an important purpose to you? Do you feel it brings you joy or carry a particular significance? If yes, we'll locate a suitable place for it. If not, we could donate it to that someone else may benefit from it."

Set the example by being an example of positivity and shining light. If you can get rid of your personal clutter, you can encourage others to tidy up also. When your table in the kitchen is filled with papers or other items On the other hand it won't be apparent if someone brings an extra lunch box or additional set of keys the pile of junk.

One suggestion that is practical: create storage opportunities by putting an "collection containers" in closets or hallways. If there's a designated area to collect clutter The clutter will then become part of a more organised thinking process. This is the first step towards eliminating the clutter!

Be positive and focus on solutions can aid in getting rid of clutter in your home and those around you. Avoid interfering too much with the process of purging others even if they seem uneasy initially. Set them an example by setting a positive permanent example someone free of the binds that comes with "too numerous things."

Conclusion

I'm sure that the tips you've gotten from this book of wisdom has been helpful to you. Clear the space for exciting new opportunities, not feel embarrassment when a last-minute company shows up to make a positive impression to your professional acquaintances and improve your financial situation and experience a feeling of calm in your own home and around the home, reduce the stress level, thus improving your overall health and well-being.

This advice will allow you to spend more time with yourself and the things you like about life. You can also consume more mindfully, and consequently be healthier, and will assist in eliminating each bad habit you have in your life.

I wish you have the best of luck in your daily life.

www.ingramcontent.com/pod-product-compliance
Lightning Source LLC
Chambersburg PA
CBHW071837080526
44589CB00012B/1028